The MADEA Factory

The MADEA Factory

Ezekiel J. Walker

The Madea Factory

Copyright © 2014 Ezekiel Walker

Cover and interior design by Ted Ruybal.

Manufactured in the United States of America.

For more information, please contact:

Wisdom House Books
www.wisdomhousebooks.com

Paperback:
ISBN 13: 978-0-616-00077-9
ISBN 10: 0-616-00077-4

LCCN: 2014907621

SOC001000 SOCIAL SCIENCE / Ethnic Studies / African American Studies
SOC022000 SOCIAL SCIENCE / Popular Culture
PER004030 PERFORMING ARTS / Film & Video / History & Criticism

1 2 3 4 5 6 7 8 9 10

Table of Contents

"This is just an illustration of a few scenes that helped raise a generation."

• Lupe Fiasco •

Introduction

Original title:

WHY I HAVE TO EXPLAIN TO WHITE PEOPLE THAT MADEA MOVIES AREN'T REAL LIFE

There are few things I, as well as other black people, despise more than having to explain our race's deficiencies and regularly fulfilled stereotypes by our own people. However, this is the foundation for why this book was written. I can distinctly remember a Sunday summer afternoon in 2011, while working at a residential treatment facility where children with behavioral issues are housed, and once again being forced to speak for the entire black race. However, this was not in defense of rap music, Michael Vick, or overpriced Jordan sneakers. On this particular day, a group of mostly white kids wanted to watch a movie and asked if I had a Tyler Perry movie for viewing. With no hesitation, I proudly said "no." I didn't reject their requests because Perry is not a decent director, but primarily because it was expected for me to have his entire filmography in my back pocket at all times in the event of such a random request. What would turn out to be more surprising to me and less surprising to the kids was that my white female co-worker of about the same age owned several of Perry's movies to watch, prompting one of the children to say, "Dang Mr. Zeke, she's blacker than you!"

A couple of hours go by and as we are watching *Madea Goes to Jail*, I look at these kids and they are loving every minute of it, especially the Madea and Mr. Brown scenes, which is understandable because after all, they are kids. I cannot expect them to watch the film for the more introspective Christian-based themes and life lessons that are a trademark within most of Perry's films. I then turn to my white co-worker and to my amazement she is laughing just as much as the kids are at the same exact scenes. Once the movie ended, the children and my co-worker began reenacting their favorite scenes from the movie, and they all consisted of either Mr. Brown or Madea's outlandish and nonsensical quotes, behaviors and mannerisms. They began to "talk black" and it became so popular that my white female co-worker renamed herself "Moniquay Lashida Lashawndra" in mockery of the overtly and unabashed ghetto nature of the film.

With all of this happening around me, many of the kids wondered why I was not engaging in the light-hearted and well-intentioned humor as well. I initially told them I was not a fan of the movie; however, they continued to probe until I finally exclaimed, "Because it makes black people look stupid!"

After that, there would be dead silence for about 5 seconds as everyone looked down realizing this was no longer a laughing matter as I had effectively killed their vibe. However, what was more surprising is the outright cynicism which would later follow from the kids and my co-worker. Many of them said, "It's just a movie. Have fun. It's not that serious."

If only they knew just how serious it was.

That was my original title and introduction to this book; however, I decided to alter the direction of the project to something more symbolic as opposed to a gimmick aimed at belittling Perry's legacy. Additionally, I wanted the reader to have the chance to read the book without expecting absurd and repeated attacks on Perry's character just for the sake of attacking. Upon further reflection and taking a second to think about the actual content of my thesis, I realized it deserved a much more succinct yet complete designation which would accurately explain the purpose of this book and hopefully intrigue the reader to learn more about the current state of Hollywood's representation of black people on and off screen.

Even when I began finalizing this book, I continued to have trouble coming up with an accurate name and portrayal of what I wanted the title to represent. I thought about "White People Do This, Black People Do That" as an ode to Dave Chappelle and to accurately describe the ever-widening dichotomy between how two different cultures can experience the same things yet draw two entirely different conclusions from it. However, throughout the title selection process, it became evident to me that this book needed to encompass much more than just a quick double-take at your local bookstore; it also needed to include and honor someone who stood for change in a real and tangible way.

In 1972, Black poet and songwriter, Gil Scott-Heron released a fictional book entitled *The Nigger Factory* in which the narrator tells the story of a group of college students who are fed up with the conditions of their school, especially its faculty and administration. This group of students presents an ultimatum to the university president which demands for things to change immediately for the betterment of the student body and for the reputation of the university at large. The university president, holding all of the power and control over the university and its proceedings, seriously considers the student activists' demands for change and actually addresses a few of the things they request. However, the bulk of their grievances go unaffected. As a result of their demands not being fully met, the group refuses to allow the entire student body to enter any of the classrooms until a sufficient agreement is reached with the university president. This act of protest effectively shuts down all learning opportunities for students and instruction for teachers. After both sides of the dispute realize neither are going to get what they want, the university president calls the National Guard on the "militant group" and there is a war on the campus, which helps neither the university nor the student body.

What I took away from Heron's story is this: while someone can have positive intentions in his/her critique of someone else or in the students' case, an institution, the method in which that frustration is delivered can make all the difference in how the accused chooses to respond. Perhaps if the student activists had not threatened the university president and taken over the campus, negotiations could have been made and discussions could have been had. Nonetheless, if a person or group is so hardened and opposed to anything beyond what they desire, there leaves no room for conversation or improvement on the very issues which need the most attention. At the time, Heron's story was very necessary and as such is necessary now, as we ought to begin the discussion concerning one of our culture's most influential and ubiquitous stars to date. Though Heron's poetry and opinions were always thought to be revolutionary and pervasive, he never once thought his purpose was mistaken or misguided based upon what he saw before him. He dissected and examined issues as they appeared to him during a time when it was unpopular and, quite frankly, unsafe to do so.

During the historical days in which Heron wrote and spoke so passionately about, a system existed which was larger than he or his cohorts believed they could possibly influence. However, now we see Perry, one of our own, perpetrating the very myths and exaggerations that Heron and other notable individuals not only argued but died fighting against. Today, Perry takes segregation which was once symbolized by torches, pipe bombs, cross burnings, and police dogs, and re-packages it into a 90 minute film featuring an illiterate character who is a grown man dressed in a wig, night gown, stockings, and lipstick. This is what I call "The Madea Factory." While the appearance of racial progression is evident in this country, characterizations such as these constantly reinforce century-old ideologies which are more redundant now than they were before.

In Heron's book, he details that while the students continue to pour their monies into the university and assimilate to the virtues of what is expected of someone earning a Baccalaureate degree, there is also a population of the student body with the knowledge that they have earned more than what they are presently being offered. The student body had brought these issues to the university previously; however, the issues had come and gone without any noticeable change. It was not until a group of students took it upon themselves to create a necessary ultimatum and carry it out that immediate action was finally taken by the university. While they were unable to instantly fix the university's issues, it was being addressed with much more purpose and intent than ever before.

Heron's book stands as a testament and confirmation for me: while people may know things are bad in a certain industry or profession, conventional or hushed-mouthed conversations do not produce the same level of results as a direct confrontation. The activists were not trying to bring the university to an end, fire the president, or create an overall mutiny; rather what they demanded was a change for the betterment of the university and its student population. They were not asking the university officials, but they were telling them. The activists understood the university to be valuable in nature as it stood to be a positive symbol in their community for young people to enter the world as adults with a better chance at life. Because the majority of the university's population consisted of black students, the group realized the university's incompetence and unwillingness to change was a result of the student body not being taken seriously. I hope to achieve a similar result with this project. I wish not to annihilate Tyler Perry or his successful career which he has worked so hard to build into the dynasty it is now. I do understand Perry and his collection of television shows, stage plays, and films supposedly represents *all things black* within mainstream America. As someone who believes those in power should be held to a higher standard, this work will reflect the following perspective: not only does Perry need to be held accountable for what he is giving to the public, but he needs to change it.

Dreams and Nightmares

"Sure, tomming was good once upon a time. That's how we got here. The old folks knew that was the only way they could raise you. What we call Uncle Tomism today was nothing but finesse and tact then. The old folks had to scratch their heads and grin their ways into a white man's heart. A white man who wouldn't accept them any other way. But at what point do we stop tomming?." [1]

"I was learning that just being a Negro doesn't qualify you to understand the race situation any more than being sick makes you an expert on medicine." [2]

• Dick Gregory •

cannot say with absolute certainty whether art imitates life or life imitates art in films created in America. During my research, I found that many of the themes and storylines from directors often stem from what is occurring in real life; for example, *Do The Right Thing*, or a fictional picture such as *New Jack City*. The former title has had more of an impact than most screenplays. In the particular case of filmmaking, it would seem that art imitates life as life imitates art. As culture dictates actions, these two things are not mutually exclusive. Hollywood directors have documented the ever-changing shifts in African American culture. From those shifts, they have also created different perceptions for the audience to look at, and in some cases, emulate.

Every time I watch a movie, I come away from it feeling inspired, enlightened, encouraged, or even saddened. It is typically an exhilarating experience. For me, the screenplays are a form of "edutainment" that I pride myself for indulging upon. I believe life needs to be balanced; in my opinion, merging entertainment and education is symbolic of that very effort. Films, much like music, have the ability to bring people together from all walks of life with a grandeur that hardly any other industry can mimic. Aside from a concert hall or a theatre room, one would be hard-pressed to find another medium where people of all colors, educational backgrounds, religions, and political affiliations can interact in a shared experience. With the power to bring people together or tear them apart, it is imperative for the director to present a holistic viewpoint of whatever he or she chooses to focus on.

If the director presents something with a one-sided or biased opinion, then he or she has wasted an opportunity to wholly make use of the platform their audience has placed him or her upon.

There is no doubt generations of Americans have vicariously lived through cinematic adventures, both fact and fiction. Movies have a way of mobilizing an audience to subconsciously think on an abstract level and become engulfed in a movie's characters, symbolism, and message. Directors have the uncanny ability to captivate the audience to the point where they may forget they are even sitting in a movie theater and find themselves existing alongside the movie's plot and characters.

As spectators, we independently absorb this information, but the message may be interpreted in many different ways, much like a painting or an exquisite piece of art. For this reason, the fact that screenwriters and directors seem to exploit the negative stereotypes associated with African Americans and pander them to a vast audience is disturbing. In addition, many of the stereotypes have strongly influenced the collective imagination in what we consider to be traditional roles for black actors, women in particular, as evidenced by the success and popularity of shows such as *Girlfriends*, *The Game*, *Scandal*, and *Being Mary Jane*. These shows stray from the overt displays of black people as intellectually inferior and often tell stories of blacks with successful careers, with questionable moral decisions, and with overly promiscuous behavior. However, it is because of their interesting and ever-evolving characters these shows are able to enjoy a long shelf life without dumbing down themselves in order to tell a story. The imagery and characteristics of persons featured in these shows help the audience relate to the characters not only because it is a black face, but more importantly, it is a black face that shares many of their same personality traits and cultural norms. On-screen characters have had an impact on the viewers for years, and oftentimes, what we see on television can, for better or worse, influence our behavior.

For example, when we see a man in the street that is dressed like the rapists or murder suspects we usually view on the news, do we subconsciously associate him with those crimes? If we see a woman wearing a night gown in the street, then do we associate her with Hattie McDaniel, Aunt Jemima, or Madea? What about a bald black male wearing a gold hoop ear ring? Do we think of Michael Jordan? Maybe. Maybe not. But an individual's pre-conceived ideas about gender-labeled garments can certainly enable them to formulate oversimplified judgments about the people who wear them without truly understanding the person, their background, and more impor-tantly, what they represent.

Again, if I were to walk outside at midnight in blue jeans, black sneakers, and a black hoody, I may be perceived as a hoodlum or a "thug," not because of my actual intentions for that night but because society has deemed that type of apparel as mischievous and unset-tling, especially when worn by a black man at that particular time of night. Nonetheless, society did not construct a fearfully judgmental attitude on its own; there have been persons of all colors who have worn this outfit and behaved in such a way as to cause others to associate that combination of clothes with anti-social behavior. However, African American men are usually held in suspicion as we have been demonized and distrusted throughout our ancestry in America.

Even in 2013, an African American male teenager purchased a $349 Ferragamo belt and was subsequently interrogated and detained by NYPD after Barney's New York staff falsely suspected the teen had used a stolen credit card. This speaks to the perception of a segment of America that will never understand what it means to be a black man in this country. Regardless of the social, political, and educational advances made by certain African Americans, there will seemingly always be this expectation of the majority of us to live in an endless cycle of degeneracy. [3]

It is therefore important for us to examine the origins of these stereotypes, many of which are expected and even embraced by movie goers, critics, and directors. The reason there are so many misconceptions about African Americans in particular is because we have been taught detrimental concepts about ourselves. We have been taught that blacks were African savages who won an all-expense-paid cruise to America from white men in knickers and wigs and who happily worked pro bono on the plantations for over four centuries. Many of us have been taught wrong from our family, school, and society, however, it is up to us to re-educate ourselves and provide beneficial information to those who are willing to learn about themselves and their history. Russian Communist Founder Vladimir

Lenin once stated, "A lie told often enough becomes truth." [3] We have seen throughout history the direct result of mis-education whether through entertainment or education and its detrimental effect it can have on those people to which it is being taught.

Having worked in the mental health and counseling field since graduating college in 2009, I have seen firsthand the results of a people who do not know their history and self-worth. Typically, when I attempted to bring these topics of race and social distinction to their attention, it would often be met with an arrogant indifference or disinterest in what was being presented. I have attended many forums, given speeches, done interviews, and there is an audience for knowledge; however, it pales in comparison to those who would be affected by a person with the stature and reach of a director. People want to be entertained and that is why we go to the movie theater; to enter a world controlled by someone other than ourselves, and we trust them to provide us with the best work they are capable of creating. Nevertheless, when an audience is continually fed a substandard product, they either become accustomed to it and therefore desensitized or, as in my case, they insist what is being presented is erroneous and let the viewers know why.

When a nation is learning facts about its history and the people who helped to shape it, important facts are frequently omitted. That is why some black people to this day are unaware of the true origins of their ancestors, the great inventors, warriors, professors, kings and queens, along with other facts and knowledge that are almost completely left out of the U.S. history books that many children read in grade school.

Our nation has been fed these lies and remained confused about our true identity for so long we have simply constructed our own sense of self through whatever remnants we had left of Africa and our present condition here in America, thus forcing many to become a "hybrid-Negro." After blacks were stripped of our names, families, and culture through Willie Lynch practices, we were left with an uncertain view of ourselves, our cultural norms, and our history. We are no longer knowledgeable of the talents, skills, and traditions our ancestors practiced and would have instilled in us if not for their enslavement. Since that point in history, the confusion of who we are has only grown and our actions towards each other reflect an absence of self-knowledge. Presently, the effects of this can be seen most clearly on the most celebrated and cerebral plantation today: television. This is where channels such as Vh1, Oxygen, Bravo, and BET display violent, sexually-crazed, materialistic, immoral, and untrustworthy characters which supposedly represent the black population.

In order to completely understand the present, one must be comprehensively informed on the past. Such is the case with all events in history; television and Hollywood are no exception. It is essential to have knowledge of those who depict the images of the past and present on screen if we wish to accurately evaluate their work from an objective point of view. Because of social media and our unprecedented access to celebrities, it has become entirely too easy to accuse someone of buffoonery or condemn their work as being devoid of substance without actually having any sort of proof or justification for doing so.

It is important to deconstruct the efforts of black filmmakers to illustrate their unique perspectives of African American culture and our world at large by using the stereotypes associated with black people. It is those very directors who have given breath to the perceptions and realities we have considered to be *normal* for so long. Incredible strides have been made to achieve independence from the stereotypical depictions of African American persons. While it was not done overnight, it does deserve to be recognized and praised in honor of those who defied the immoral norms America has become accustomed to and continues to fight desperately to keep intact. In addition to mentioning the strides of our country's black filmmakers, we must also recognize the current shape of the industry's most popular and profitable films.

This book was instrumental in allowing me to take a comprehensive look at African American film culture and gain an increased appreciation for it. As a product of the mid-1980s, I cannot honestly say our generation can relate firsthand to the minstrel shows or early 20th century films like *Birth of a Nation* that once stigmatized blacks and marginalized us without due justification as the stereotypical depictions are now much more calculated and incognito.

Additionally, I aim to stress the importance of a specific African American director, the frequency in which he produces films, the types of films, and what the last twenty years predicts for the future of our film culture. This is not an attempt to thoroughly discuss each film which has had an impact on American culture and influence, but rather to better highlight the perceptions and realities of African Americans which films and characters have created over time. It is also not an attempt to critique movies as a professional but as an educated viewer and admirer of African American films.

One glaring reality I will also point out is that in some instances, our own people have become brainwashed and returned to portraying some of the very stereotypes and inaccurate portrayals of African Americans we once denounced.

"There is a tendency in America to denigrate intellectual development and education and to gravitate towards instant gratification of sensationalist media . . .

. . . So that's the problem, and the Black community is the victim of this dynamic, as is the white community and the Latino community, all communities in America are in the grip of this media—not disease, but epidemic . . ." [5]

• William Greaves •

This contemporary epidemic is a topic which many black directors have already expressed to be disheartening. For example, cultural critic Manthia Diawara condemns *Birth of a Nation* for portraying blacks as savages, rapists, performers, and inferior in every human context. [6] While every example may not be that extreme, the fact remains there was either a missing perspective or an existing fallacy in Hollywood which galvanized blacks to direct movies which were only accurate according to his/her individual interpretation. What many of these black directors have in common is their disgust and disbelief for the images they have viewed on the big screen, thus noticing an immediate need for change. Being a black director in a traditionally white Hollywood is something that has proven to be a challenge over the years. This book will uncover the notable figures that have contributed, in one way or another, to the societal expectations of black films and black people.

Whether it is true or not, blacks are believed to be hedonistic and therefore do not ascribe to the notions of higher learning, intellectual discovery and new experiences. This notion of higher learning can take shape in many forms such as exploration in the arts through mediums of film, music, paintings and other forms of artistic expression. If there is no diversity in the various forms of art and culture which are presented to the masses, then the biased and unimaginative works will continue to be produced and propagated as truth. Whether the public has become used to these works or due to the artist's comfort zone and inability to produce anything else of substance, it is clear that without a change, audiences will continue to be robbed of experiences, and the director's creativity and range will continue to be limited. There has to come a time when we ask ourselves, is this because of old Hollywood stereotypes or is this due to the current imagery of black life to which we are exposed daily? What is the driving force behind this national anti-intellectualism which is inexplicably magnified when speaking of African Americans?

This is not merely a plea to America to begin reading books again, but rather it must be understood how and why we have shunned the very efforts of those who seek to edify our world. We may never discover how we have reached this point; however, it is important to understand the implications of allowing our culture to remain this way. If there is a lack of improvement in not only the words we read but in the images we see, we cannot expect any creative developments within the images of film portrayals, particularly those which coincide with black culture.

A director is often faced with the all too familiar conundrum of catering to substance or style in his/her delivery. Does one produce commercial films in the hopes of reaching a mass audience through hedonistic themes, vague story lines, and repeated scenarios? Or does one produce a work which may not be directed towards a mainstream audience, yet moves them beyond the expectations of his/her already loyal following? I would imagine it can become a difficult decision to make, especially when one recognizes, for example, that *Avatar* grossed over $2.7 billion in lifetime sales as of February 2014.

To put it into perspective, Tyler Perry, while he is clearly the biggest black filmmaker of all time, if you took the gross profits of all of Perry's films, you would still need three times more money to reach *Avatar's* $2.7 billion worldwide earnings. It is clear, for many reasons, Perry is not on the same level as director James Cameron, and I am sure he has no desire to be, but this illustrates the disparities in Hollywood in regards to funding, casting, production, and marketing a particular film. Traditionally, in various industries across our nation, black people have not had the type of financial backing and support system of their white counterparts, and filmmaking is no different. It is a fact that it is harder for a black person in America to acquire funding for certain things, whether it is a movie or a home. According to *Inquisitr*, *The New York Times*, and multiple other news outlets, Wells Fargo, U.S. Bank, and Countrywide Financial are a few of the banks found to practice unethical loans, and in some cases, violate federal anti-discrimination laws. Bank of America, in 2013, was found to be practicing unethical housing restoration jobs, leaving foreclosed homes in minority neighborhoods to rot, while their white foreclosed homes would be well-kept, resulting in a $335 million lawsuit paid out by the Bank. [7]

A film such as *Avatar* with no real controversial messaging and universal appeal would attract most movie goers as it is a film which may leave one feeling exhilarated from the 3-D experience and innovative graphic designs. The intertwining storyline between war and love, accompanied by futuristic animals and people, creates an unforgettable experience for movie goers worldwide. By having the ability to produce films which appeals to the masses, it dramatically decreases the risks to be undertaken by the director thus highly increasing his/her chance of gaining profit from the film and creating more works of his/her choosing.

In our ever-changing world of instant gratification, entertainment, and even education, has changed dramatically. The decline in readership from the traditional paperback or hardcover book to the now more preferred eBook is most notable. [8] The way our country intakes its information is completely different than in past decades; people are less likely to read a book in the traditional sense. I discovered this reality upon releasing my first book. In my experience, there were plenty of people who were not only skeptical of a new author but who also scoffed at the idea of having to sit down and read a book.

In my aforementioned first title, I spoke candidly about the apparent stereotypes of African Americans, both the obvious and the incognito. In this book, you will find many of the origins and causes for said stereotypes. The reason, at least in my estimation, for these labels is to easily categorize persons whom an outsider does not truly understand or relate to. A more scholastic definition of stereotypes may be "psychological representations of the characteristics of people that belong to particular groups." [9] Entertainment produced in Hollywood—unlike any other medium—allows the viewer to experience something that can change the perception of all persons who witness a powerful film and/or accept a character's beliefs, ethos, or motivations for doing ultimately good or evil. It is the creation of age-old stereotypes which gives life to the cultural expectations, moral or immoral, that we all have for one another.

One of the more common stereotypes is usually known as "Uncle Tom." The name is derived from Harriet Beecher Stowe's fictional book *Uncle Tom's Cabin*, which was originally released for mass production in 1852. The story describes a male slave who has been institutionalized and brainwashed so heavily that he loves and adores his white master and would vehemently defend and support him and his family without question. This character is largely based upon the consequences of enslavement and is often depicted as beyond loyal, and most importantly, submissive to the welfare and whims of his white master. While "Toms," for short, were ubiquitous and considered normal only a century ago in American film, the role of that character has developed into something we can only subtly witness in today's film and television.

Earlier in the television mini-series *Roots* (1977), a character named Fiddler, the elder male slave, advises the incoming slaves of the rules and regulations of their new master. Fiddler, consistent with his "Tom-isms," tells the new-comer, Kunta Kinte, not to rebel or run away and also informs him that, "if he is good to massa, massa will be good to him."

Now obviously "Toms" had been brainwashed, like most slaves were at that time, to love and protect the interests of his master at all costs, even if it meant turning his back on his own people. However, even Fiddler would joke around with his "co-workers" at his master's expense—something that would have been an anomaly earlier in the century. Nevertheless, what gave the "Uncle Tom" a sense of pride was the delusion that he was valued by his master. The fact that his master noticed him doing good and occasionally rewarded him for his good behavior was all the motivation he needed to maintain his undying devotion to a man who told him when to work, eat, sleep, and if/when he could reproduce. What we call "positive reinforcement" today is the only thing an "Uncle Tom" needed to feel sufficient and quite frankly, it may have been the only thing which kept him from being castrated, whipped or even killed. After being institutionalized and de-programmed for such a long period of time, "Toms" and other slaves began to remember very little of their origin, but rather only what they had been told by their master, thus creating a sense of reliance and dependence on the very system which had captured them. In Carter G. Woodson's *The Mis-Education of The Negro*, he makes this point excellently:

> *"If you can control a man's thinking you do not have to worry about his actions. When you determine what a man shall think you do not have to concern yourself about what he will do. If you make a man feel that he is inferior, you do not have to compel him to accept an inferior status, for he will seek it himself. If you make*

a man think that he is justly an outcast, you do not have to order him to the back door, He will go without being told; and if there is no back door, his very nature will demand one."

Indulge me for a moment and allow me to think as a 19th century white man who owns black people as chattel.

"Hmm . . . I like Tom, he does whatever I say, makes the other slaves do what I want, he doesn't talk back or challenge my authority in any way. But now I'm bored. His back is no good after picking all my cotton for the last twenty years. If only Tom could jig . . ."

Now we find another common stereotype which most people have heard of, in some form or fashion. This "coon" caricature is one of many fascinating stereotypes. Later in this book, I will examine one of the most celebrated, if not the most celebrated "coons" in American History, Stepin Fetchit. For now, let us examine the makings of a perfect "coon," as it was celebrated in the early 1900s.

There are mainly three types of "coons;" the first we will explore is the "pickaninny." This particular "coon" caricature was usually a child who served no other cinematic purpose other than to provide comic relief to the drama which was occurring within the more serious storyline. One of the past generations' most popular examples was *The Little Rascals* token black character, Buckwheat. His bulging eyes, wild and unkempt hair, along with his overly simplistic perspective created a caricature which was wildly embraced in both the earlier film (1955) and the latter (1994). This adolescent "coon" is someone who grabbed the attention and fascinations of mainstream white American movie goers who were still divided over the idea of free Negros existing in "their" America. Hollywood, knowing that fact, blended two things people still love today: children and humor. It was a perfect recipe for success—take a group of people whom you really do not understand, degrade them by only offering roles you think are acceptable and proliferate them amongst your equally ignorant and conservative audience as dim-witted and simple-minded. Nothing said "safe" like an innocent and clumsy black child, and it was the "pickaninny coon" who made mainstream white America laugh and ultimately accept young Negro performers at a time when blacks were widely labeled as subhuman and inferior.

The second type is the "pure coon" who is crazy, unpredictable, often lazy, and slurs his speech sometimes beyond recognition. Robert Townsend did a masterful job of displaying this in *Hollywood Shuffle* (1987) where he portrayed the 20th century minstrel legend Stepin Fetchit. These old school "coons" were often shown stealing chickens, eating watermelons, gambling, or performing as nothing more than a side show to the more pertinent and ultimately important characters and storyline.

Another important extension of the "coon" is the "Sambo," one who is perpetually a child in an adult male body. He is completely incapable of taking care of himself and his entire existence is in his master's hands. "Sambo," never one to complain about the conditions of slavery, oppression, or mistreatment, was used as a counter argument to the system of slavery—using the foolish logic which stated if a slave does not complain and he is loyal to his master, then the system is working fine and needs no repairing.

Tyler Perry has modernized this caricature with "Mr. Brown" as he embodies this child-like black man whose sole purpose is to be laughed at, if by nothing else, his appearance alone.

The last type of "coon," according to author Donald Bogle, is the "Uncle Remus," who is less apparent and obvious to the eye of the normal "coon" characteristics. The "Uncle Remus" understands his place and does not desire anything outside of his comfort zone, he is more like the "Tom" because he sees no reason for anything to change as his naiveté and institutionalization has completely overcome his entire sense of freedom and self-respect.

A third stereotype, that was much more apparent and blatant, is the female "tragic mulatto" character. She is "tragic" in being the overly dramatized character and "Mulatto," which according to Merriam Webster, even today means, *"the first-generation offspring of a black person and a white person."* Individuals such as the very beautiful Lena Horne were considered to be in this class of racial labeling during the prime of her career from the early to mid-1900s. However, Horne was just as socially aware of her status as she was gorgeous—refusing to play the very stereotypical roles both mulattos and blacks were known for at that time. Horne not only disagreed with the direction of African

American roles but she also worked with the NAACP to help erad-
icate the very prejudiced system by which she was being employed.
Her mulatto complexion and body frame were admired by both white
men and women; however, it was her uncompromising stance against
being defamed for the pleasure and ultimate approval of whites which
crippled her career in America. Horne would find more roles and longevity abroad as America was unwilling to compromise its stance on
the perceptions of black performers.

The "tragic mulatto" was favored by massive audiences; even
audiences in the South, who were not in favor of films that did not
specifically cater to their racist ideologies, were intrigued by the
character. She was beautiful, fair-skinned, and usually an emotional
wreck. This was a winning recipe for directors, casting agents, and
producers of Hollywood who believed the only way a black woman
could be beautiful is if she is mixed with white blood. Often the tragic
mulatto is portrayed as a victim or an image of sympathy whom is
never fully happy and always seems to be troubled by her personal
relationships. The "tragic mulatto" moved white audiences towards
the entertainment realm of theater to see a near white actress perform
with her white counterparts in an unfamiliar role that often involved
romance and the luxuries of a life denied to that of her darker and
heavier antithesis, "Mammy."

The "mammy" or "Aunt Jemima" caricature is usually seen as a
descendant of the "coon" and "Tom" characters. Nonetheless, what
distinguishes "mammy" is a slight sense of independence which

affords her the opportunity to occasionally backtalk her masters and think for herself, something which is rarely witnessed coming from early black caricatures. Another characteristic of "mammy" is her appearance; she is usually dark skinned. If the actress was not dark enough, at times she was given shoe polish to wear on her already black skin. The "mammy" was also portrayed to be very heavy. Again, if the actress was not heavy enough, she was given padding to appear larger than she was or forced to eat excessively to gain weight. [9]

"Mammy" hardly made any form of commentary regarding sex or intimacy, as she was created to look hideous to the audience, which therefore stripped her of sexuality and whatever potential love interest she may have had. "Mammy" always loved her work; she loved working for master and his family and making sure they were all living well. She worshipped God more so than any other caricature; she prayed and sung religious spirituals while cleaning and preparing food for her master, doing his laundry, and tending to his children. There was a silent and sometimes explicit understanding amongst the black women and children that whites were the superiors; constantly pray to God for survival, and if you want to keep your job, you must too perform your duties with an endless humility, an unbroken loyalty, and a forced smile.

As if blacks had not been marginalized enough during that time, they were also banned from performing on stage in certain cities, prompting local whites to mimic and mock blacks on stage using shoe polish on their faces, or what it is better known as "blackface."

Later, after the Civil War, blacks were largely required to use blackface in order to perform. Louis Beavers, who made the "mammy" caricature famous in *Uncle Tom's Cabin* (1927) trained herself to speak more slowly and plain, in order to appear more southern and simple-minded, however, she was from Cincinnati and spent time in Los Angeles, neither of which resemble the southern style of dialects that movie presents. According to author Donald Bogle, as proof of the forced lies and manipulation perpetuated by Hollywood, "during filming, professional white cooks had to prepare the food. Then Beavers was situated at the stove, smile intact and pancake flipper in her hand; thus the image of the jolly black cook was completely manufactured and presented for mass consumption." [10]

When we look at a mammy of the old days and look at Madea today, many similarities can be found. Whether it's their sassiness, nightgowns, devotion to God, desexualized nature, "ebonics" or "blackface" which Madea has modernized by using makeup, we find that the image we see today is nothing new but instead a recycled version of the mammy caricature.

This groupthink went far beyond the "mammy" as it appeared in *Mandingo* (1975). In this film, a female slave was prepared by her own mother to lose her virginity to her master, as he had ordered it as casually as a pizza from Domino's. As she was visibly upset and crying, her mother effectively told her to do as he said and to enjoy it. If this was the system in place, then who were they to challenge it?

In reality, "mammies" had families of their own, with whom they were deprived of spending time. They could not assume their motherly duties because they were busy taking care of a white woman's children on a full time, sometimes live-in, basis. A major distinction the "mammy" and "coon" share is their happy-go-lucky demeanor, which again reinforces the falsity that slavery was not so bad and not only did blacks enjoy being unpaid servants but they also gained pleasure from serving their white master and his family. A more recent and less overtly offensive depiction of the "mammy" in Hollywood was featured in *The Wolf of Wall Street* wherein the actress serves as Wall Street multimillionaire Jordan Belfort's in-house maid. She also serves as one of three black persons in the entire film, all with minimal speaking roles. One black male serves as a maître d and another in an infomercial testimonial. This is hardly the diversity of character roles one would expect from a major blockbuster film released in 2013.

The last stereotype to be mentioned is the "Buck" or the caricature occasionally referred to as the "brute." Beginning in 1915 with D.W. Griffith's *Birth of a Nation*, this adult black male caricature was born and distinguished by his brutality as a result of being sexually repressed, which in turn made him into a sexually starved belligerent man walking around looking to do nothing but wreak havoc on anyone in his path. They were often depicted as savages, lustful, and somewhat animalistic; "bucks" were a reminder of a runaway slave, in that they roamed freely and wildly with nothing to lose and everything to gain. The characteristics were comparable to and reminiscent of Nat Turner, who put the fear of God into the hearts of whites and was able to be re-packaged throughout the years for mass consumption with personalities such as a young Mike Tyson, O-Dog of *Menace II Society*, and 50 Cent in his early rap career.

In *Mandingo*, there is a level of acceptance for the norms of slavery, which inevitably includes abiding by the master's whelms and wishes. In this film, "Mede," played by Boxing legend Ken Norton, goes through his life with an "Uncle Tom" brain in a "Buck's" body. Over the course of the film, Mede is responsible for the death of two black men, one of which is a runaway slave whom he ferociously chases down at his master's request and is hung afterward. He kills the second man in a "Mandingo Fight" his master places him in. Mede, even after being sarcastically praised by another slave for being the master's favorite puppet, never once second guesses his master until his life is being threatened by that very master. Fellow slaves try to enlighten him on the fact that he is literally being used to kill other black men; yet and still, he is content with his role on the plantation. In this particular case, Mede is a hybrid Tom-Buck character who maintains the physical strength of an ox with the mental awareness of a caterpillar.

The only thing, according to Hollywood depictions, that could quench the thirst of a "buck" was the flesh of a white woman. Again, this played to the fears of a majority white audience by falsely reinforcing white women as the lustful and innate desire of every Negro male, a temptation he supposedly could not resist. This is something Mede would be confronted with during his time at the plantation that would ultimately lead to his murder by his own beloved master's rifle. Most recently, the more savage and animalistic "buck" was seen in the 2011's *Rise of the Planet of the Apes* where an ape, along with others, were locked in cages in a museum. However, the biggest and scariest of these apes, aptly and brazenly named "Buck," was given a cage of his own and isolated from the other apes. He possessed the characteristics of a violent human "Buck"—freakish strength, unpredictability, an outcast even amongst the runaways—and most obvious, he was angry and black.

NFL audiences were introduced to this caricature in January of 2014 during a post-game interview. Seattle Seahawks' cornerback Richard Sherman, who was demonstrative and abrasive in his celebration, screamed passionately into the camera at an opponent he had just beaten for a chance to go to the Super Bowl. The viewing public had been taken aback by the enthusiasm and aggressiveness of Sherman, especially when noticing he was being interviewed by a blonde white woman. Many viewers drew conclusions that Sherman was a "thug," and it would prompt him to later apologize for his actions. The interview lasted for no more than twenty seconds; however, America would talk for over a week about race, the black male plight, modern athletes' responsibility to fans and children, the "angry black man," and what it means to be a "thug" in America. In the greatest of ironies, this conversation was had during the immediate aftermath of the game on Martin Luther King Day. What this modern example of a "Buck" proved is: while America believes it has progressed so much further than the Civil Rights Era, moments such as these verify very little has changed in the perceptions and visualizations of certain African Americans. America, over time, has proven it only accepts blacks in the images they feel comfortable with and not how we individually choose to be. Throughout time, blacks have found it nearly impossible to be themselves without compromising the authenticity and morality they owned prior to entering their field of choice.

Birth of a Nation is one of the most infamous screenplay examples of the hatred, ignorance, prejudice and incendiary propaganda which fueled the beliefs and belligerence being spewed from whites during its era. It was such a controversial picture that upon its release, protestors, including the NAACP, successfully removed several grotesque and exaggerated parts of the film that were only made to further denigrate blacks. All the same, the remaining stereotypes within this film kept such ideologies alive and well in its final script. In June of 1915, the Ku Klux Klan burned down a street in Atlanta, Georgia to celebrate the film's opening. Later in the year, on Thanksgiving Day, members of the Ku Klux Klan rode their horses on Peachtree Avenue. Ed Guerrero, author of *Framing Blackness*, mentions that black people had every right to be afraid because the images of the film were coming to life in this instance, hence differentiating a movie from reality was nearly impossible. This movie is the only reasonable starting point for a discussion of stereotypes in American film, for it embodies the cause and effect of distributing something so propagated, offensive, and polarizing that both races of audiences react to it with either a sinister embrace or a vociferous objection.

Many of the stereotypes we now see in Hollywood are a blend of past misconceptions. One of the most obvious of these is the 2009 release of *The Blind Side*. A major box office success, *The Blind Side* tells the story of a real life impoverished black high school football player who, when his crack-addicted mother and absent father are out of the picture and he is out of options, is saved by an assertive, wealthy white woman. While the circumstances of his upbringing are neither his fault nor the fault of the woman who helped him overcome his homelessness, recidivism, and illiteracy—it is a familiar storyline since the days of chattel slavery, and early American films which often depicted an ignorant black youth who is civilized by the well-rounded and wholesome white family which represents everything that is courteous and noble. A master could buy a number of slaves, and depending on a particular slave's work ethic, personality, or at the master's discretion—become that master's favorite. One of the most disturbing facts about slavery involves the slaves being stripped of their African names and given the last names of their master. This predicament is something Civil Rights legend James Baldwin spoke about at length in a 1968 documentary entitled *Baldwin's Nigger*.

Not only were slaves given their master's name, but often times they were taught how to be civil through their master's lifestyle which included religion, diet, social gatherings, patriotism, family, business matters, etc. Masters provided slaves with an entirely new methodology of how to live and operate in their new world. After slavery, this would further develop into avenues such as sports and entertainment with whites providing blacks with opportunities to use the "skills" they acquired on the plantation to translate into entertainment for the silver screen or the field. *The Blind Side* attracted attention because it was reminiscent of the traditional adoption of a disheveled, disadvantaged black male into the warm, loving arms of a new white family who taught him the fundamentals of life, just as their ancestors had done generations ago. The only contemporary difference is that the circumstances created by slave owners are now seen as box office attractions that can make white Middle America feel more cognizant about the plight of the modern American Negro, without having to act on that awareness.

There were many cases of the NAACP protesting films which crossed the boundaries of entertainment and only depreciated the American-constructed identity of the black race. Blacks, determined to disprove this myth, began creating their own films in the early 1900s. Oscar Michaeux, the first African American filmmaker, proved for the first half of the 20th century that a black man could direct films and have longevity in Hollywood. Nevertheless, his run was, and in some respects still is, considered to be an anomaly for black directors. Though Michaeux and others had good intentions, they did not experience the level of box office success which would sustain their self-respecting roles and direction. Ultimately, whites would re-assume their role of pop culture and black culture arbiters.

Stereotypes of black men have been pervasive and damning for centuries, yet we do not endure this plight alone, as women have also struggled with detrimental manufactured stigmas as well. Melissa Harris-Perry, in her 2011 publication, *Sister Citizen: Shame, Stereotypes, and Black Women in America*, highlights the stereotypical shaming of black women being promiscuous and hypersexual which "justified the sexual abuse of enslaved women" and later "their involuntary sterilization." In the 1960s, a group of wealthy American citizens, including Dr. Clarence Gamble of Proctor and Gamble and James Hanes of Hanes Brand Clothing, served as eugenicists who believed "poverty, promiscuity, and alcoholism were traits that were inherited. To eliminate those society ills and improve society's gene pool, proponents of the theory argued that those that exhibited the traits should be sterilized."

North Carolina, my home state, was one of the 31 states to participate in this nefarious ethnic cleansing program. Most of the sterilizations were performed on young girls under the age of 18, with some victims being as young as nine years old. [10] Instances such as these illustrate just how little a human life is valued in the eyes of those who arbitrarily decide to play God by determining who is allowed to have children and who is not. This eugenics program would exist in

North Carolina from 1929 to 1974; for nearly fifty years, women and young girls were being sterilized, largely without their knowledge or consent of what permanent damage was being done to them.

Additionally, the black female body was often on display and made to appear as accessible as a bail of cotton, especially during slavery. Oftentimes, black women were stripped to naked during slave auctions, while working in the fields, or when being whipped by their master. These examples were then seen as normal characteristics of black women having a healthy libido; however, when they continued to be reinforced for so long, it became accepted into our nation's culture without question. Over time, society no longer questioned why women were continually categorized as objects, only to be trusted with sexual pleasure. During slavery, we see how lies were used to rape and impregnate black women and later restrict them from having children without their knowledge. This type of propaganda, while nonsensical and without justification, has had a lasting impact on our country, the way we look at black women, and what we expect from them. The most visible examples today are the many characters of reality shows whom are often dramatic, lustful, and more importantly, unfit to be a wife or mother.

This book was not written to demean Tyler Perry's work but to show that he, above all others, has had a profound and pervasive impact on his audience, both commercially and relatively—both black and white. What is more important than judging his work as the gatekeeper of all things black is to remind ourselves that no director has, nor ever will have, the ability to speak for the 20+ million black people in America. It is impossible and unreasonable to have such high expectations of one person with his or her own story to tell.

The story of rags to riches is not an unfamiliar one, particularly for African American culture. As frequently reported, many of the persons we admire who also receive international acclaim were once struggling to a point where they hit a crossroad and all they literally had left was their talent. Tyler Perry, being homeless at one point, surely motivated himself to utilize his skills and life experiences to build a dynasty as large as it currently is today. There had to be moments when he felt like giving up or second-guessed his vision, especially while performing in front of only a handful of people, but it was ultimately due to his relentlessness and the support of the people that validated his dreams. We have to be willing to support the persons who are trying to make a difference, and if we do not, we have no reason to complain.

The purpose of *The Madea Factory* is not to highlight the lapse of social activism within the last thirty years; though it is apparent things have changed regarding what Hollywood provides its consumers and the bleak expectations of its audience. There is a clear and unchallenged status quo that was once comically ridiculed; nevertheless, those depictions are what is most popular among moviegoers currently. The Wayans, more than anyone in recent entertainment history, have tried to dispel the stereotypes of black people through *In Living Color*, their TV show, and the various movies they have contributed to, so we cannot truthfully say blacks have not attempted to address and repel the imagery created by persons such as Perry. I think the bigger question now is: Does anyone care?

While I have spoken with many readers who expressed to me they continue to read books because they enjoy the escape and the learning experience which can take place upon discovering the unknown, I have also met an equally large number of individuals who dislike reading and asked if I could provide them with an audio book. Reading requires time, abstract thinking, and in many cases, a formation of one's own opinion; it is something many people simply do not choose to engage in. As our younger generations are continually utilizing the latest technological advances, it is no wonder asking them to read a book seems outdated and far-fetched. This is the reason movies have proven to be so pervasive in American culture for so long, because they present a way to provide a visually stunning image and detailed story with an immediacy most books cannot match. When a large segment of our population is accustomed to only reading one hundred forty characters at a time written by people they choose to follow on Twitter, it highlights a precedent the rest of the edutainment world must acknowledge and either conform to or fall into an obscure existence which is the distinction of many who have failed to adjust with the world's "evolution."

Movies offer the audience a chance to experience a different perspective, through the lens of a character that we, the audience, may not relate to yet we contrive a sense of appreciation for their story of survival, humor or drama. What other element in our society offers such a gratifying element of art, propaganda, style, and theme in such a succinct and aesthetical format? There's a reason the movie industry flourished during the Great Depression; it offered an escape from the gloom and despair which defined that period of time. The artistry of filmmaking is woven into the fabric of our country and has proven over the years to influence our trains of thought well beyond the theaters, even filtering into our personal lives. For example, a large segment of the population decided to name their new-born children after the popular Sci-Fi/Drama *Twilight* series characters, Jacob and Isabella. Let us also remember the strategic creation of products which go into popular films, such as the latest James Bond film, *SkyFall* (2012), where Heineken reportedly spent $45 million to be included in the movie in addition to their television and digital campaign. [11] *SkyFall* would also feature automobile makers such as Landrover, Audi, Beetle, Range Rover, Jaguar and Aston Martin. The film used a Sony laptop, an Omega wristwatch, a Tom Ford suit and sunglasses, and a Walther PPK pistol. [12]

These examples present evidence that the cinematic experience we have become accustomed to is methodically designed to remain with us long after the film's ending. The big screen can leave indelible marks upon our lives—including what we eat, vote for, buy, believe, drive, wear, everything! It is due to this subculture of film that I have come to recognize the various motifs which exist within African-American film. All in all, we have become consumers of not only brands, but fictional depictions, and it is important to note the types of brands our people gravitate toward and ultimately engulf ourselves in.

The impact of film in our culture, for this particular book's purposes can be drawn back to the aforementioned 1915 *Birth of a Nation*. It is a film which grossly depicts blacks as savage, dim-witted, and mentally delayed entertainers while whites are depicted as heroic, law-making and trail-blazing hooded Klansmen. It is true many of the movie's over-the-top depictions were confronted and challenged by whites and blacks; however, the power in which that film influenced America at large was symbolized after its release. The movie's impact was pervasive not only for citizens, but even President Woodrow Wilson commented on *Birth of a Nation* with ". . . And my only regret is that it is all true." [13]

The picture also illustrated a confirmation concerning what the nation equally thought of blacks and whites. Whatever preconceived notions and stereotypes in question were emphatically answered in this film; there was no room for interpretation. Once the audience absorbed this movie's theme, blacks subjected themselves to an archetypal model of peonage while simultaneously creating the new standard for blacks to degrade themselves to on the silver screen.

This film's success would categorize and label blacks for the next half century and simultaneously enrage those who knew the images being presented were not reflective of their authentic identity. There was a vehement backlash; notwithstanding, in the racist society of the 20th century, capitalism was still very much alive. *Birth of a Nation*, as one of the most controversial and technologically groundbreaking films in American history, was accepted by mass audiences as they rushed to theaters to support a movie that would denigrate American Negros for decades to come. A more infamous example of a flabbergasting TV series is *Amos 'n' Andy*, which created hysteria across the country amongst African Americans viewers. It was originally constructed by two white men, Freeman Gosden and Charles Correll, who mimicked so-called Negro vernacular and produced a radio show in Chicago in March of 1928 that would eventually become the longest running radio program in broadcasting history at the time. They would later take their success to the television screen and receive backlash and protest from viewers who detested their extremely offensive mockery of black people. So offensive in fact it would prompt the NAACP to take action by releasing a Bulletin entitled, "Why The Amos 'n' Andy TV Show Should Be Taken Off The Air in August of 1951" which stated,

1. It tends to strengthen the conclusion among uninformed and prejudiced people that Negroes are inferior, lazy, dumb and dishonest.

2. Every character in this one and only TV show with an all Negro cast is either a clown or a crook.

3. Negro doctors are shown as quacks and thieves.

4. Negro lawyers are shown as slippery cowards, ignorant of their profession and without ethics.

5. Negro Women are shown as cackling, screaming shrews, in big mouthed close-ups, using street slang, just short of vulgarity.

6. All Negroes are shown as dodging work of any kind.

7. Millions of white Americans see this Amos 'n' Andy picture of Negroes and think the entire race is the same. [14]

In the case of *Amos 'n' Andy*, white men created and portrayed the actors as foolish and second-rate schemers, even though blacks themselves had already played these roles "successfully." So we see that the perpetuation of negative black stereotypes is something which was persistently reinforced throughout the decades. Even though most black actors had already given up those typecast roles, the culture of Hollywood and America was still hungry for more wide-eyed and simple-minded slapstick comedy routines that would be intentionally recreated by white people if black actors were unwilling to do so.

While this example is a television series, the common theme of blacks being depicted as fools, that so many people once loved and looked to preserve, is nothing new in America. However, now it is the younger generations who are absorbing the descendant traits of that time. Though the "coonery" is not as overt as it was years ago, black people are still carrying the weight of the compromising characterizations that their predecessors had to portray in order to advance the race's status and respectability in Hollywood.

White People Do This, Black People Do That

"The dilemma of the Negro actor still exists. He is perplexed, two audiences, white and black. What shall he do if he wants to move to higher things?" [1]

• Clarence Muse, 1934 •

n the long and celebrated history of American filmmaking, there have been numerous roles filled by a vast array of characters from an even wider pool of selection. From action films to romantic comedies, Hollywood is responsible for delivering some of the most memorable and impactful moments in our history. It has shaped the way we see each other and how we ultimately choose to treat each other as human beings. There is no doubt that because of Hollywood's influence we associate certain groups of people with wealth and authority while we see others as poverty stricken and distrustful. While certain stereotypes may have some source of truth or myth, when these generalities are broadcasted and in some instances, celebrated, the message can be manipulated and presented as a condemnation without explaining the root of said stereotype.

I can remember watching Saturday morning cartoons as a kid and seeing images of black people eating watermelon or chicken with a jamboree playing in the background. At the time, it was merely a cartoon giving me the entertainment I desired. At no particular moment in the cartoon was I called a "nigger," "spook," or a "monkey," yet the images of these distinctions were being presented to me and millions of kids who were glued to the television. By using these nefarious and subliminal messages, entertainment outlets began to poison, and have continued to poison, the minds of American society of what it means to be black in America. Now this is not to suggest a Saturday morning cartoon is solely responsible for the current status of black people, however, it does illustrate the conniving and reprehensible method in which these myths are perpetuated.

Entering a field that has historically been dominated by a traditional system and power structure is the challenge many new artists find themselves engaged in. It is not until someone with charisma, talent, passion, and an unwavering message comes along that things are shaken up enough to make a notable difference in their field and consequently change the way messages are presented and interpreted. Artists, of all types, experience this at some point in their career, and directors are no different. One notable example would be that of director Charles Ahearn, who in 1983 released the film, *Wild Style*, which offered an inside look at the new hip hop phenomenon that was rapidly growing amongst New York City's young black males. It also highlighted individuals such as Jean-Michel Basquiat, who could not only produce works of art on New York City subways but also in the finest art galleries in the world.

When speaking of the way films were financed, the cliché rings true that times have truly changed from then to now. Melvin Van Peebles was once asked how he was financially able to create *Sweet Sweet Baaaadassss Song* (1971). His response was: "Put a couple chicks on the block, raise the money and make a film." [2] Can you imagine a director today saying he paid for his film through prostitution? That film would never receive any sort of credibility; profitable agencies for the welfare of prostitutes would oppose him and ultimately shut down such an enterprise with a press conference where a blonde white woman tearfully explains why this movie offends her so deeply.

There are plenty of Hollywood stereotypes which construct the racial and social expectations of our nation. There is a reason Sandra Bullock grabbed her purse when a couple of black men approached her at night, and there is also a reason they consequently robbed her. While *Crash* of 2004 was used to shine light upon the stereotypes which exist in our country, it also proved those stereotypical depictions needed much more exposure than one film can provide. I am not necessarily advocating for a reformation of Hollywood's themes and characters, but if there was a concerted effort towards shedding light upon different aspects of diverse persons, it would add more perspective than what already exists in the minds of many movie goers and Americans. Hollywood studios are able to exhaust a stereotype, negative or positive, until audiences begin to accept their propaganda as unquestionably true. A more extreme and well-known historical example of this occurred during Hitler's reign of terror in Nazi Germany; he constantly spewed derogatory and propagated messages throughout the country as a way to inundate the Jewish people with a complex of inferiority. It is believed if you spread a message long enough, people will begin to absorb it regardless of its connotation.

Diversity in filmmaking is so important because as seen in 2013, with the fall feature of the film *12 Years a Slave*, it exposed how Christianity was manipulated to validate and incessantly enforce slavery.

There are scenes of white masters reading scriptures to their slaves and explicitly telling slaves if they are disobedient to their masters, then they are in turn being disobedient to God in Heaven. While it is saddening yet true, this film was the first depiction of slavery to be directed by a black man, Steve McQueen, who expertly highlights the differences in how various cultures and individuals choose to examine the most damning period of our nation's history. Without his perspective on religion, a vast audience may not have thought slavery and religion were so intermixed. Upon viewing the picture, it is impossible to separate the two. It was important for McQueen to illustrate just how brainwashed slaves had been by documenting the inundating nature of Christianity during their enslavement and the profound mental handicap that slaves were taught to have.

There are certain things catering to the "African American Experience" that cannot be accurately documented on-screen by someone of another race. Regardless of how many persons, of any ethnicity, have seen a movie based on the slavery in the antebellum south, there will always be a level of disconnect because for them it is simply a movie, but from a black person's viewpoint, these things are a historical reminder of how we arrived at the current position we find ourselves in.

When watching *Roots* and witnessing the dissension that exists between "field niggers" and "house niggers," anyone can understand the concurrent interactions of light and dark skin slaves based upon their treatment from the master. For a black viewer, these traits continue to exist in everyday life in regard to relationship preferences, corporate advertising, and imaginary expectations from both black and white viewers. When someone of another ethnicity learns of the dissension between black skin tones, they may come to believe that while it is unfortunate blacks were separated and discriminated against solely for their tone, they would also imagine the insidious nature of those days have long passed, not realizing such idiosyncrasies have continued to permeate our society to this very day. Many viewers would not perceive how the world's most popular and visibly influential black persons, women in particular, are of a lighter shade, serving as a reminder that the closer an individual exhibits European physical features, the more beautiful and trustworthy that person is considered to be. As mentioned before, this is significant to a black person who has been educated about his/her history and understands its connection in their daily lives. However, it is not enough to simply be knowledgeable of a subject, but a firsthand experience is what provides black directors with the proper context of how to present a subject, such as the effects of a light or dark skin tone, because he or she has actually lived it.

I would imagine it to be difficult for an expert to write on a subject in which he/she can only provide content to as a spectator, as opposed to those who have lived and experienced such events. It is a common grievance of the coaches and players of professional sports teams, when at the end of a hard-fought game, a reporter later questions their decisions in regard to why they did not win a game or series, as if they know more about the game being played than the actual participants who have prepared their entire lives to play the sport. Not only is it naïve to think they could offer some sort of advice, but it demonstrates the arrogance of one who thinks because they may have spoken to someone who has encountered this experience firsthand, that they now have the credibility to critique the decisions and outcomes of someone or a group of people who have actually contributed to something outsiders can only talk about.

Black people understand the distinctive influences which have helped us reach our current position in society, and such influences are not incomprehensive, as they are historical and remain prevalent today. We are a group comprised of many personalities with many different motivations, and it is due to this reality that it must be understood, there is no one answer for the plague and plight of black people but a collective view of our history must be observed to understand our current standing in the world.

If one were to examine the images presented to us on the big screen by Perry, or even commercially on television, an outsider may assume these two things are mutually exclusive. However, the personalities, ambitions, and ethics of most black people could not be any more intertwined with reality. Black people are born into more adverse circumstances than any other ethnic group in our country; no matter the amount of wealth or status we have established or have been provided with, we understand life is not going to be easy and there are certain expectations to live up to from outsiders and each other.

In knowing that we have a shared experience, which cannot be truly understood by anyone else outside of our race, the pressure of someone who assimilates to the heights of Perry must be daunting, as he has fought so hard to reach this pinnacle of ingenuity and owner-ship of his brand and its messaging. Nonetheless, when it is analyzed and critiqued for quality and accuracy, there is much to be desired from Perry's work.

Consider the different aspects of African American lifestyle; con-trary to popular belief, some people are born into wealth, the middle class, and as widely believed, poverty. With that being said, we all have differing perspectives of not only the world but the culture of the world. As an affluent person, no matter how many times one par-ticipates in a charity event or feeds the homeless, there will always be a part of their own people that they, through no fault of their own, cannot relate to. On the contrary, take someone who grew up impoverished and saw their family struggle to eat and keep the lights on, there would be a disconnect between them and someone who has never had to decide whether to spend their last few dollars on gas or food. You see, we are all different and have innumerable experiences that make up our personality, ethos, and expectations; there is no one "Black Experience," just as there is no one "White Experience." The United States is a country filled with persons of differing traditions, families, and motivations, and it is because of this, we are divided by choice yet united by a common purpose driven by capitalism with aspirations for success, and black people are no different. Having been denied the most fundamental rights for so long, black people have been playing "catch up" for over fifty years.

Due to the limited view of blacks in America before having our own filmmakers, the result was an extremely desensitized view of blacks, for men in particular. However, now that we have been able to see a number of black directors translate their own experiences to audiences, we are currently seeing motifs recycled and replayed under a new name as the messages remain the same.

Most people create their adult beliefs and preferences based on what they have learned as children, we then use that mindset to shape our future decisions. The only difference is how one decides to expose his/her life. Most people do not release these beliefs and preferences because they either move on or choose to leave traumatic events in the past. However, there are some who decide to confront those issues head-on, in an attempt to present their very unique and sometimes unprecedented view of their world. At times this is met with controversy and other times it is met with praise; nonetheless, it is essential to have persons from different socioeconomics, states, affiliations, and personalities who can offer something that we, as people, have not experienced before.

Realistically speaking, it may be impossible to shine light on an entire race's issues. The more persons we have who can offer something new adds to the fact that there are people out there with different perspectives and talents who can portray their own version of reality through drama, action, comedy or hybrid versions who can speak to the life experiences of an entire audience.

Another major challenge of black directors is comparative to the expectations our culture deems everyone to maintain once they have reached a certain altitude unexpected by their peers. To "keep it real" or "100" as I understand, is to not only remember where you have come from but also to report on what you have seen as immoral in your world and to do your best to change it with your newfound platform. When someone escapes an environment where problems are obvious and often ignored, the community then becomes dependent on that individual to carry the load of their grievances in order to shed light on the problems the wider and mainstream audience may be unaware of or intentionally disregard.

That is a challenge which many black people, including directors, have to confront—especially when considering African Americans have been historically disenfranchised in this country. There is a sense of obligation to the cause of being the race's public representative, not necessarily to exploit our shortcomings, but to tell stories of individual experience, as opposed to merely presenting an onslaught of statistics. To humanize the very people whom are normally described on the news as criminals, thieves, welfare recipients, and intimately dysfunctional is something that can typically only be done by persons who can relate to their community firsthand. Once directors are able to illustrate how families are affected by epidemics such as crack cocaine, absent fathers, violence, poor education, unhealthy diets, and poverty—it can offer a face to what is usually reported as another disturbance in a bad part of town. Directors have been able to offer detailed stories which are able to stay in the minds of audience members far longer than any news clip could ever hope to do.

The malicious Rodney King beating of 1991 proved to confirm the suspicions many Americans felt about the police and the judicial system; it also shed light on the violent struggle of blacks against whites, the once authority of a slave master over a slave. After watching that horrific display of overt gang violence, it became apparent that no other officer intervened to tell the officers what they were doing was criminal in and of itself. It revealed to the public that such behavior was acceptable and had been for some time; the only thing more disgusting is the verdict of innocence undeservingly given to those "officers of the law." That incident divulged to many Americans that the "good ol' boy" system is still in place to protect itself at any cost, no matter how evident the criminal action. Consequently, the streets of Los Angeles saw some of the most violent attacks and riots in our nation's history. Persons who were sick of being taken advantage of rose up and executed justice the only way they knew how which left an imprint on our nation, revealing there is only so much unwarranted punishment an already "minority" population can take.

At a time when gang violence and drugs overcame the streets of Los Angeles in the 1990s, this example of extreme police brutality gave the world a look at the corrupt system of oppression and marginalization existing here in America.

The Rodney King incident is also reminiscent of the 1960s riots across the nation, where the patience of the inner city individuals finally ran out, as they expressed their frustrations by showing the only way to be recognized is to demonstrate "civil disturbances." It is necessary to remember that during this time period, Dr. Martin Luther King Jr. was assassinated. As a result the non-violent movement was losing its appeal and the once pervasive influence of "turning the other cheek" became an afterthought. How else can one stand up against a system that has consistently obliterated their people since bringing them to a distant land? After trying to live peacefully and abide by the laws of the land, black people saw no other option but to retaliate with force. That period of time marked a defining moment in our country's history, where a large group of people came together to revolt. While many were arrested and killed, they made a statement that they would not accept the arrogance and blatant shamelessness of the U.S. judicial system. After listening to their leaders, organizing protests, marching for just causes, witnessing their brothers and sisters beaten and killed, for many blacks the only thing that made sense was a rebellion, for it was the only option they had not explored as they now had no true leader.

Robert Townsend, in *Hollywood Shuffle*, parodies the life of a young black man trying to make it through Hollywood's racially compounded web of expectations built by those who only have a second hand account of what it means to be "black." Townsend comically exposes the deliberate tactics of producers, casting agents, and directors to transform a self-respecting black man into a "Tom," "Buck" or "Sambo." Townsend mentions how he drew upon his own personal experiences as a young black actor in Hollywood going through the typical best friend or "token" roles. He and Keenen Ivory Wayans wrote the script for *Hollywood Shuffle* and the film is a representation of adjectives usually devoid of most past and present main black characters—smart, hard-working, humorous, and self-aware with a love interest that supplements his career focus. As a testament to their dedication to this particular film, they notoriously ran out of money in the middle of shooting, and went on the road to do stand up in order to earn money to complete the film; Townsend would later charge the remainder of the film's costs to a plethora of credit cards.

The Wayans Brothers opted to take Hollywood stereotypes and make them their signature as much as a swoosh is to Nike. The Wayans family produced TV shows such as *In Living Color, The Wayans Brothers* and films such as *White Chicks* (2004) as well as multiple other pictures—all of which takes time to mock racism and show just how idiotic all of our expectations are for one another. From movies like *White Chicks* or the much earlier film *I'm Gonna Git ya Sucka* (1988), the Wayans family has made tremendous strides in confronting race humorously—more so than anyone else in Hollywood over the same period of time. It demonstrated one of the cleverest ways to combat and mimic serious prejudices and ethos which comprises the very fabric of America and made the viewing audience realize how petty and ridiculous some of our beliefs are, often times enabling them to laugh at the notion that some of us actually believe in them.

Other films such as *Coming to America* (1988) were instrumental in providing a comedic performance from a young Eddie Murphy, Arsenio Hall and Samuel L. Jackson. This movie is what I would imagine a conversation between Marcus Garvey and Richard Pryor would have sounded like. From Prince Akeem's bath of every man's dream to his oblivious nature in Queens, NY, the barbershop conversations, "Sexual Chocolate," and "Soul Glo"—this movie was not only an instant classic, but its lingo and characters have lived far longer than anyone could have predicted.

Many themes of black movies are either based entirely on reality or complete fabrication, which is why it is of the utmost importance for one to have the ability to discern fact from fiction. One should know that in *School Daze* (1982) there were and still are black sororities in existence which have a "lighter is better" perception in regards to one's skin tone, and though the movie is fictional, it is based on the authentic events of both Historically Black Colleges and Universities as well as American views as a whole. Whereas if one looks at a film like *Meet the Browns* (2008), there is no basis for the film's mockery and exaggeration of the actors, in particular its main character, Mr. Brown. It is paramount to have a foundation of what's most socially pressing or topical, especially when one is representing a large majority of persons in their viewing audience. If the work is anything less than authentic, it stands out like a *Who Made the Potato Salad* (2006) or *The Cookout* (2004).

This seemingly endless battle between substance and saturation has been waged and debated for decades. Perhaps it is less than an endless battle, for a battle consists of two opposing sides in a confrontation to which the victor achieves their reward for entering the fight in the first place. This goes for war, politics, taxes, sports, almost any facet in which a person or organization has the right to oppose another's beliefs or actions. This same battle occurred on a more urgent level in the days of civil rights and segregation, as was provided in the NAACP Protest of *Amos 'n' Andy* illustrated earlier. However, I believe the most disheartening difference from then to now is the fact that it was clearly whites who were performing as dumbed down blacks and those performances served no educational, cultural or social purpose for the people their shows were mocking and profiting from.

I cannot help but wonder whether the character of Madea or Tyler Perry would have been acceptable in those days if she were played by a white man in blackface, or for that matter would a white director be accepted today in making Madea films? In 2007, former

MSNBC radio host Don Imus, who is Caucasian, called female African American players of Rutgers University basketball team "nappy headed hoes." Immediately after, there was uproar from all sides of the media, social commentators, and non-profit groups which successfully demanded Imus be removed from his position. Undoubtedly, the term "nappy headed hoes" is offensive, regardless of whom it comes from, but can we realistically think that if it came from Perry or a black person of influence, their job would be threatened by a multitude of viewers and media personalities? I truly believe if Perry's films and caricatures were produced in the middle of the 20th century, they would have indubitably invited protests, backlash, and potential riots because of its inaccuracies and insulting manner. The color of the two actors skin is why *Amos 'n' Andy* was taken off the air and it is the same reason that today Tyler Perry is a successful entrepreneur and mogul, leaving us to conclude that racism, when it comes to comedy, is only skin deep.

As a people, we must raise the standard to which we are willing to support a person's work. That individual must earn their right to our dollar, our vote, and our validation. We have to demand more of those cultural arbiters and what they deliver, to not only us, but outside viewers who may not understand the nuance of the message being presented. We the consumer are primarily responsible for the content created by any industry of entertainment. Perry would not make Madea films if no one watched, just as the NFL would not show games on Sunday, Monday, Thursday and Saturday, if there was not a starving audience waiting for their next fix. If we are unable to demand more of the persons we anoint as spokespersons, then we take on the responsibility of verifying that what they represent is indeed valid and an accurate representation of our views. This is no different than any local politician who represents a district of civilians who elected him or her. With every ticket that we buy, we continually validate Perry and what he represents.

On the surface, it looks as if we are all, black or white, going to see a movie, but in reality, as a viewing public we know what we are going to get when we decide to view a Madea film, and it is our complacency with his films which have assisted him to become the most profitable black director in history. The themes and motifs featured in his films, in particular the black male characters, can be related to stereotypes of violence, distrustful, and immoral; all of which are characteristics that were once believed to be true of all blacks. All in all, like most entrepreneurs who can learn people's behavior and provide them what they want on a consistent basis with little variation over time, Perry is brilliant.

It is no different than what Coca Cola established in 1886 by creating a dominant brand in the beverage industry. They introduced Diet Coke, and later Coke Zero, but no one is mistaken, the original Coca Cola was and still remains the money maker for the brand.

Coke can manufacture dozens of flavors in the future, but they never will discontinue what originally made them rich and famous. This goes for Perry as well; he can make dramas, movies about marriage, and pictures catered to "colored girls," however, Perry knows what galvanizes his audience to enter the theater and it is not himself as an action hero, or even Idris Elba as a responsible and caring father. Tyler Perry Studios, like most other corporations, may have felt pigeonholed by the success of his early years and thought it necessary to expand his brand and product. While his films may receive positive, and sometimes negative feedback, it does not dictate or rebrand the product; it is merely a sample of another direction the company is capable of producing, and it is up to the paying customer to decide whether the new product is worth their loyalty as the original was.

It is up to us, as the audience, to decide whether Perry's work is worth our "co-sign" and if we continue to decide it is, as we have thus far, we must to accept the consequences of these pictures. Just as our nation accepted blacks as ghetto, violent, inherently aggressive, and misguided because of the 1990's direction of filmmaking, we must once again lower our standards for blacks in America.

Shine On

"America tried to emasculate the greats,
Murdered Malcolm, gave Cassius the shakes, wait
Tell 'em rumble young man rumble,
Try to dim your lights, tell you 'be humble.'" [1]

• Jay-Z •

The Madea Factory

For decades, America was dominated by ultra-conservative stances which permeated the country at large, and as "old habits die hard," America was reluctant to change its views of anything remotely considered liberal—including rock and roll music, marijuana, and the true freedom of black people. In the earlier part of the 20th century, blacks were still struggling to gain the equality and status that was granted to them in the Emancipation Proclamation of 1865. Our country, the South in particular, was slow to respond to the government's new legislation and enforcement of the new laws that would prohibit the sale of blacks as property and effectively shut down the "good ol' boy" system that our country was literally built upon. With no education and a newfound freedom, many blacks had no choice but to work on the same plantations they were once enslaved at, but for a small profit this time. Much like modern times in the southern states, whites created legislation they believed would benefit them politically and socially through creating racially biased voting laws that were much more blatant back in those days.

The mood of our country's conservative ideology was something so pervasive, many of Hollywood's directors and producers simply would not make a film that showed blacks as independent-thinking persons. They were intimidated by the South's culture of hatred for blacks and believed if they were not portrayed as inferior, it would turn the South, as well as the nation, against them and their movies would flop—so instead of making films offering remnants of a respectable people with knowledge of themselves, they showed the polar opposite image, and that translated at the box office.

This conservatism has remnants of Alabama Governor George Wallace infamously stating, "Segregation Now, Segregation Tomorrow, Segregation Forever." The Red Summer of 1919 was a time when black people were mercilessly slaughtered across the country throughout the hottest months of the year. This period of time also includes the ridiculous Tuskegee Experiment which began in 1932 in which black men were injected with syphilis until 1972 in order to examine its posthumous effects on the body. There was the 1963 church bombing, killing four "colored" girls in Birmingham, Alabama on a quiet Sunday morning. The perpetrator, Robert Chambliss, would be originally found "not guilty" until a later FBI investigation in 1977 which brought forth more evidence to convict him and send him to prison where he would die in 1985. The March on Selma of 1965 would expose its grotesque local police force; they were determined to disallow blacks their right to protest what they believed to be an unjust murder of a fellow activist, Jimmy Lee Jackson. During this march, a crowd of roughly six hundred protesters were dispersed as they were gassed and beaten by police forces, state troopers, and horse-mounted officers.

It is because of these and many other unforgettable instances that it became so difficult for blacks to progress in the entertainment mainstream and on most Main Street's across America. There were challenges many had to confront which may have gone unnoticed by the mass American audience. Because of the conservatism of our nation, evolution was made nearly impossible, and no one expected black people would evolve past the imagery that was beyond their control. Blacks, as we all know, became "sick and tired of being sick and tired" with the status quo and rose up to orchestrate change on their generation and all of those whom were willing to follow. [2] It seemed that conservatism was only beneficial to those who were in power, and America was content with waiting for the times to catch up to the equality of which blacks were in immediate need. The struggle was seen most consistently through the marches, protests and sit-ins, where blacks and whites were beaten, and some were even killed, in the process of creating liberation for all its citizens.

Many accomplishments of the Civil Rights Era are credited to the most famous persons involved in the movement such as Martin Luther King, Jr. and Malcolm X. According to some, these persons divided a nation into two parts, but both wanted the same thing: equality. However, more individuals than the ones most prominently noted helped to integrate the American public. Two of my favorites are Comedian Dick Gregory and Activist James Baldwin. Gregory, a legend in his own right, used comedy to bridge the tensions and injustices that were ongoing during the Civil Rights movement. Gregory was also important in that he was and continues to be a thought provoking and in-depth personality who is able to tell intelligent jokes and interject necessary social commentary. Gregory, even today, uses his experiences for comic relief and political activism to illustrate how fundamentally egregious America's racial denigration of blacks is.

James Baldwin, in my estimation, is one of the greatest orators of our time. Not only did Baldwin stand up for racial injustices but he did so with a distinguishable eloquence, grace, and fervor other speakers and demonstrators could not dare to match.

The benefit of Gregory is he could be funny about serious issues facing our nation's growing hostilities, whereas Baldwin confronted these issues with a more prophetic and poetic approach. This is not to suggest Gregory was not dedicated to the cause, as his arrests, prison hunger strikes, and 1968 campaign for President of the United States provides proof of his commitment. Comedians have the ability to project, dispute, and speak their minds with seemingly no filter, and it is that same unabashed style which made Dick Gregory a legend and helped to pave the way for his successors, such as D.L. Hughley and Chris Rock.

Later in the 1970s, when Ronald Reagan was elected President, there was a rebirth in the conservatism and classic Americana culture as he would finish the job of his predecessor, President Nixon, by attempting to rid America's inner cities of drugs. Reagan would also develop economic policies that disproportionately affected African Americans and defined his legacy in the eyes of many who lived through that era.

Reagan represented everything that was beautiful to white America—his looks, guns, and movie star status propelled him into the favor of the American people and represented everything that many blacks despised as another stereotypical depiction of a white man in power. Along with "Reagonomics," a system purposely designed to discriminate, incarcerate, and oppress blacks, Reagan continued a tradition of black denigration so disastrous that anyone living during the era still talks about it to this day.

Later, "militant" Negros would surface and cause the U.S. government to fear black progression and the "by any means necessary" mantra which soon became synonymous with young blacks in the 1950s and 60s. The uprising of revolutionary geniuses such as Malcolm X, Fred Hampton, Gil Scott Heron, Huey P. Newton, Stokely Carmichael, later known as Kwame Ture, James Baldwin, Eldridge Cleaver, Bobby Seale, and others created a shift in the cultural dichotomy which stressed black self-determination and equality across the board. There was an emerging class of resolute individuals who grew tired of the discrimination, hatred, and inferiority complex American society attempted to designate for the Negro; they demanded that people notice their contributions to ending this disgraceful and manufactured blemish within the fabric of American society.

The word "revolution," in American culture, is often regarded as a bad word. Often times you may hear "revolt," "protest," maybe even "upheaval," as euphemisms for what is actually taking place. There have been revolutions since the beginning of human existence; however, the definition in an American perspective, has been altered. Not to be elementary in this explanation, but the difference between revolution and evolution is more than one letter. Let us suppose blacks wanted "evolution" in order to end slavery and oppression, I would probably be picking cotton instead of writing this book.

Evolution reminds me of the time-sensitive word "eventually," and while certain things need time to mature and grow, others have to be confronted without delay. You see, evolution is a natural process of things happening without the influence of an outside source whereas revolution occurs when an outside source decides to impose its will, whatever it may be, on the current situation to effect a subsequent change.

The emergence of Spike Lee, Melvin Van Peebles, Oscar Micheaux, and other black directors represents the revolution of black filmmakers who grew tired of witnessing something that constantly represented inaccurate portrayals of their culture. They decided to use their talents within the arts to effect change for African Americans. It is not to say their impact is any more or less pervasive than that of Malcolm X or Martin Luther King Jr., because all these men shared the objective to make the public more aware of the travesties which confronted their people. I would call all of these men revolutionaries because if they had not stood up and expressed their vision, whether through film, literature, or speeches—the public would have been denied a rare glimpse into a culture they may have not understood fully. While many of them underwent scrutiny from not only mainstream America but blacks too, they created an awareness and consciousness that was absent in the more peaceful and politically correct period of filmmaking.

For years, Negro Americans saw what the result of their passivity would be: the continuous and seemingly never ending unapologetic discrimination, segregation, beatings, and killings. Blacks were not seeing significant results from the 1865 Emancipation Proclamation, and therefore, many chose to rebel against a system which had mistreated and abused them for long enough. While America may be one of the more progressive societies in the world, we too, have our prejudices and biases, which are often based on perception and pure ignorance. The debated controversy of gay marriage, for example, which has been a hot topic for the last two Presidential elections, will one day be made legal, and years from now people will look back and question why it took so long to become lawful.

We ultimately live in a progressive society, and that does not mean any and every fetish or outlandish form of behavior or trend should be accepted. However, it does mean we have to recognize unfaltering shifts in culture, and if we are unable to do so, how can we really say we are more forward thinking than the Middle Eastern countries we are programmed to fear and distrust? Just as whites marched and died with blacks during the Civil Rights movement, I too support the right for anyone, regardless of sexual preference, to be married. Though I may not engage in their practices, it does not mean I cannot be supportive of their rights as American citizens. Imagine if Hispanics had no support in their fight to bring forth a comprehensible and enforceable immigration reform plan; what if they had to fight their battle alone against the U.S. government? It is the diversity of supporters that gives their fight legitimacy and relativism amongst some Americans who only see their struggle through the camera lens of someone who may or may not have any political stance or ulterior motive.

Take the arts and filmmaking for example, Spike Lee utilized a platform which has been used to belittle blacks for years and repudiated that notion into something positive, in-depth, and personal for many of his viewers. He did what his ancestors did years ago in the "Big House," taking scraps from the Master's plate and turning it into something that could feed their own families and in some cases, prepare it better than they did for their masters. It provided black directors with an "equal opportunity" to respond to those false accusations through their own life perspectives. Whether it was the parody of Robert Townsend's *Hollywood Shuffle* or the "head nigga in charge" persona in many of the Blaxploitation era films—blacks responded masterfully with authenticity to the fallacies that personified white fantasies about what black culture should look and sound like.

Many commentators and black scholars have denounced Perry's films, mainly because they provide a view of African Americans reminiscent of the days of Stepin Fetchit, who in the early 1900s played a variety of "coon" caricatures, even earning the moniker of "The Laziest Man in the World." While Stepin Fetchit's name was also fabricated (titled "step in fetch it"), he was also an educated man who wrote for the *Chicago Defender* for many years. In addition to the high quality coonery of Fetchit and Perry, they both have also enjoyed unprecedented financial success as a result. Fetchit, during his career became the first African American actor to become a millionaire. Similarly, Tyler Perry has also broken every opening weekend or ticket sales previous African American directors maintained—all while selling a message of buffoonery which was thought to be extinct.

This system of oppression and marginalization far exceeds film and can be traced as far back as our arrival in America. Centuries later, persons such as Louis Armstrong and Paul Robeson had to dumb themselves down in order to appease a white audience whom only accepted blacks for being inferior, docile, and quite frankly, simple. This form of systemic image restriction and controlled character motifs would be most prevalent in the works of Sidney Poitier who seemingly always represented what black audiences hated most: a black man manufactured by white Hollywood. Poitier was heavily criticized throughout his career for succumbing to the pressures and expectations of white audiences to present a non-threatening and asexual black man.

In *Lillies in the Field* (1963), Poitier's character, Homer Smith, catered to the whims of a German nun, he reluctantly obliged her requests to fix her home and build a chapel for their community after finding himself stuck in their new town. His character was adamant about leaving that town upon his arrival, but the mother nun's insistence and manipulation kept Smith there much longer than intended. During his time there, the other nuns were clearly smitten by him; however, there was no genuine love interest which is to be expected in a movie role involving Poitier and other black lead actors at that time. He also introduced the nuns to southern gospel rhythms they were unaware of before, simultaneously ingratiating himself with their conservative small town culture and proving himself to be a happy-go-lucky Negro with a southern soul and sensibility.

Along with the later roles of blacks serving as asexual and non-threatening on-screen characters, in 1989 the world was introduced to Hoke Colburn, played by Morgan Freeman in *Driving Miss Daisy*. His character was a man who tolerated a snobby and barely older Jewish woman named Daisy Werthan who thoroughly denigrated his value and worth during the film. Daisy's beloved "mammy," Idella, served as the typical sassy dark-skinned unattractive and fat housekeeper audiences could relate to just as older crowds could recognize from earlier in the century.

The fact that blacks have continually been relegated to portraying inferior roles and stereotypical characters is not a new revelation. In fact, a majority of roles have improved across the spectrum that Poitier and Freeman's roles helped to pave the way for. Blacks are now slowly seeing a multitude of platforms and branching out to different roles. Even while there is always room for improvement in our culture, we have to acknowledge the strides made thus far to expand the roles and opportunities afforded to blacks in Hollywood. A popular and often contentious example of a modern black actress breaking the mold is Kerry Washington's character, Olivia Pope, in the drama *Scandal*. While Olivia is a savvy, sexy, and smart black woman, she is also a manipulator, mistress, and is often distrusted by those closest to her. She, at one point, had a black boyfriend, for whom she would later break up with for the President of the United States.

This is the problem with the stereotypes I have identified earlier in this book. Washington's character is a woman who exhibits intellectual superiority along with an equally passionate emotional longing for another man. These two things were often separated during the early days of black actresses who were only given supportive roles which required them to look attractive and not contribute anything to the storyline or main character. Kerry Washington as "Olivia Pope" demonstrates she can be as physically attractive as she is cunning. Because of her current role and its popularity, it reinforces how a black woman's role should not be subjected to such a narrow and predictable palette of caricatures, and by keeping her in this nominal place, you would deny the audience an opportunity to see the range of abilities and specialties black women have already been denied to exhibit for too long.

There has been a culture of nonchalance which has permeated our country for centuries in regards to the life and death of black men. The value we came into the country with has left us long ago and it is because that value has been erased, we ourselves have grown up in this country not fully understanding our rich and incomparable historical lineage. Once castigated as secondary and utterly mean-ingless, that mind frame encouraged white Americans to enslave us; however, it has also contributed to the regression of experiences and expectations of one another. Our expectations have become so low-ered and marginalized, over time our sense of normality has departed and we now know only what has been told to us, rather than what we have actually learned or experienced. We are living based on what is expected of us and not from what we know to be true. As a result of us living out a fallacy based on someone else's ideology and myths, we have in turn adopted those very nonsensical beliefs for ourselves, judging both ourselves and others based on this lie of inferiority/ subjectivity. If one were to make parallels and take away the results of this mental and physical enslavement and denigration, it is clear the powers that be would prefer black masculinity to be obliterated, by any means necessary.

When I say "black masculinity," I speak in terms of everything that makes a man what traditional society deems as "manly," such as being a responsible father and husband, looking and dressing like a man, speaking clearly and confidently, and controlling his own destiny. To examine the personality traits of the common man today, it has been redefined by society's recent acceptance of homosexuality so now, black or white, it becomes difficult for a man to identify with himself because married gay men and women will soon have the same rights as straight couples. With this acceptance of gay culture, we have seen them too become exploited in the media as sex crazed, misunderstood, and discriminated against as blacks have been and in some cases, continue to be. Nevertheless, a black man is not required to be gay in order to be subjected; blacks have been relegated to a lower stratosphere in our country regardless of their sexual orientation or economic status.

It is rare to see a black man on television who is not serving as some sort of entertainer and the joke or sidekick of whatever the storyline could be. Oftentimes, black men are subjected to portray these roles for the same reasons as before, they are not seen as essential parts of a story or script, and therefore, their presence and opinions are not always needed and are easily dispensable. This may seem like an insignificant part of television and movies, however, when you think of the totality of these things, coupled with the fact that America has historically went out of its way to ensure blacks were not seen as equal, it becomes evident this is no coincidence.

Let us take today's most influential movie stars, Will Smith and Denzel Washington. Will Smith, while respectable and well-deserving of every accolade he has earned, is not scaring anyone and has represented the American Dream since becoming a household name. Early in his career, Smith performed this "rite of passage" by dressing up as a woman and being as silly and unassuming as past minstrel show performers were. This is not to suggest Smith ever resembled a "coon" caricature in the least, but it does point out he has represented what white America thought a black man should look and sound like: safe, charismatic, and always happy. Even starring in *Ali* (2001) would not change the overall perception of Smith as he demonstrated his acting range and the diversity of roles he is capable of mastering. Denzel Washington, for as many spectacular and indelible roles he has performed in his career as a respectable, independent, and confident black man, he himself only won an Oscar for his role in *Training Day* as a crooked cop and co-star to the more noble and pristine white rookie cop Ethan Hawke. Within five years prior to the *Training*

Day release in 2001, Washington had powerful roles in *Remember the Titans* (2001), *The Hurricane* (1999), *He Got Game* (1998), and *The Preacher's Wife* (1996), none for which he would receive an Oscar.

Even in the cases of the most financially successful, supremely gifted, and commercially marketable black actors, we see how even they have had to endure obstacles similar to their predecessors in regards to recognition for their talents and the biased view of how they are celebrated by the pseudo arbiters of Hollywood films. Even though Smith and Washington are mega stars, they are not exempt from the historical plight of slavery and the residual effects of it today. They both have seen how the system is played out firsthand from the perspective of international celebrities; conversely, it is often those who do not have the acclaim who suffer most.

This is why Trayvon Martin and Oscar Grant were killed without any valid provocation or reason. A black man cannot be seen with any sort of self-respect, honor, and culture as he chooses to define it or else he is immediately deemed problematic and in need of immediate elimination. The same reason those two young men were killed is the same reason Tyler Perry wears a dress: America is not accepting of who we are as people. This translates accurately from the bum on the street corner to the President of United States. At the end of the day, to some people, we are all just niggers. In the process to eliminate the stereotype and the struggle which comes along with it, persons such as a Tyler Perry create this happy-go-lucky caricature which removes all semblance of what it means to be a Black Man in America. He strips himself of dignity and replaces it with a wig, stockings and nightgown all in the name of acceptance. Acceptance from his peers, audiences, and whoever will support him, for being a man who adopts the appearance of a woman, which symbolizes his disconnect with everything a black man is. To continuously perpetuate the myths and fallacies created against us for popularity and profit reeks of shame, disgust, and betrayal to those who attempt to overcome the constant barraging of negativity and misguided assumptions.

The danger in what Tyler Perry is doing through his Madea caricature is reinforcing a lie which should have never been told initially. There was never a valid argument that black people were dumb or mentally inferior, it was simply fabricated to justify enslavement.

National stories such as Emmett Till, Rodney King, Sean Bell, Oscar Grant, and Trayvon Martin made us all aware of the continual false perception of black males' intentions, as the public continues to galvanize persons of authority to take their lives without reason and often without penalty. Many of the attempts to dispel the stereotypes mentioned thus far have had bleak and non-apparent results. In the next chapter, it will become clear how black people responded when they were able to finally project their own visions and stories.

Someday We'll All Be Free

"Kenny Lofton you feelin' my pace?
They only care 'bout a nigga when he stealin' the base
It's like I'm Wilt the Stilt, I'm fuckin' them all
They only care 'bout a nigga when he dunkin' the ball
And it breaks my heart
The world's a stage, I'll just play my part." [1]

• J. Cole •

The 1973 film, *The Mack*, proves the influence a film can have on American society. In a scene which presented the best pimps in the country at the annual "Player's Ball," the movie's main character Goldie wins the award based on his nationally revered excellence at pimping, voted amongst his contemporaries. Up until that point, this event was based entirely on fiction and had no authenticity. However, once it was released, there has been an annual Player's Ball which was solely based on *The Mack*'s contribution to film, black culture, and its own brand of urban renewal. Not only did the film present black men as self-sustaining, independent thinking "entrepreneurs," but it also provided them with a stylish and grandiose fantasy of the pimp lifestyle.

Though the 1983 film *Scarface* was not directed by an African American, it has affected more of our lives than director Brian De Palma could have ever expected and has remained the *go to* movie for young African American males in particular. Its apparent cultural hypnosis has been seen most profoundly by rappers of the past two decades. *Scarface* created a blueprint that would be carried on for many years after, evident in films such as *King of New York* (1990), *Belly* (1998), *Hoodlum* (1997), *Paid In Full* (2002), *Shottas* (2002), *New Jack City* (1991), *Dead Presidents* (1995) and many more that emulated his story of "nothing to something, by any means necessary." As mentioned by Ace in *Paid In Full*, "it was like niggas love seeing a poor ass Cuban just blow up to be the man, all by himself." At that time, *Scarface* proved, to many young black men, that success was attainable; all you have to do is be a Cuban immigrant, start off as a political hit man, "network" effectively, become an underboss and then through numerous shoot outs, cocaine binges, and after killing your best friend—You've made it! Easy right? Sometimes I wonder if these admirers of *Scarface* ever watched the film to the end.

It was puzzling to me how so many of us loved *Scarface* and would fantasize about living the life of a gangster who never trusted anyone. However, it is not hard to see how we became engulfed in this culture. We as African Americans have often associated with persons we see on television or movie screens, oftentimes even if they are completely different from ourselves. Because it is so rare to see a black person on the screen, we gravitate towards them regardless of their role. Hip hop, which is the most pervasive form of entertainment in our culture, is often utilized as a conduit to what is new, cool and respectable in American society, especially towards the youth. When we see rappers from Jay-Z to Chief Keef speak of Tony Montana's influence in their lives, we react with an incessant appreciation for that rapper's preference.

It is an apparent cultural delusion, as most Italian films do not feature African Americans and have frequently relegated or downgraded their contribution to American history, as referenced in *Do the Right Thing* (1989), *Goodfellas* (1990), and *A Bronx Tale* (1993). Films such as *Casino* (1995) and *Donnie Brasco* (1997) are also commonly referenced in our hip hop culture as examples of the definition of entrepreneurship, succeeding against all odds in a usually violent or conniving scheme designed to get them to the top. It is because of these films that we, as an impressionable people, identify ourselves through their characters decisions and worldviews.

In years past we, ourselves, have identified with both Martin Luther King, Jr. and Malcolm X, two men representing a similar struggle yet offering different views of how to emerge out of that very struggle. Fast forward nearly thirty years later and we see rappers Notorious B.I.G. and Tupac Shakur are involved in a struggle for a common purpose and subsequently both are killed as well—all while blacks across the nation are living and dying by the very ethos those leaders used with a microphone to deliver their messages. These two talented rap artists never saw the age of 26, and the Civil Rights legends Malcolm X and Martin Luther King Jr. never had a 40th birthday. While their relationships with each other were nowhere as hostile, they both were cut short of their opportunity to shine their brightest lights on our country's biggest tragedies and see the result of their hard work and dedication to the empowerment of their people.

When a people have gone so long without accurate representation and the only image they have of themselves is negativity and inferiority, any message showing them in a positive light is usually embraced and shared amongst members of that culture. However, this is where that population must be able to decipher the difference between propaganda and reality. Once a culture understands propaganda is being used against them, it is ultimately up to them to set the standard for what is to come of their people in the future and what they are willing and unwilling to accept. This change has taken longer than projected.

It was due to the history and culture of Hollywood that a precedent was set for black actors to follow; there was a recipe for what it meant to be black that was uncompromising. Though black people were much more involved in film at this point in history, we were still under the control of a system which had profited from depicting us how they saw fit.

> ". . . It was the discovery that I wasn't Black enough for Hollywood. So here I am from the projects, ten kids, Tuskegee, my whole world was Black, and I get out here and I'm not Black enough." [2]

> • Keenen Ivory Wayans •

Being "black enough" was something that was in high demand in the 1970s; once segregation and the subsequent Civil Rights Era dissipated, blacks became more expressive than ever. Not an entity to let anything go without publicity, Hollywood capitalized on the opportunity to produce exploitive films of blacks in what would later be known as "Blaxploitation."

This era was, if anything, a reflection of black attitudes and happiness with being able to finally think and act without the barriers Hollywood had on them before—at least that was the idea. Black people were able to direct, produce, and star in their own movies with the themes reflecting their individual or group perspectives. Even though some of the films were flagrantly and embarrassingly bad, the fact that we were free to express a different theme than the typical servitude, shuck-and-jive picture the audience had become accustomed to was a much needed relief. With that newfound freedom, we saw many different types of films which diluted the stereotypical depictions once thought to be accurate portrayals of blacks. During this period, there was no tap dancing, wide smiled, big eyed, "darky" to entertain "massa" and his audience. This was the polar opposite of that time frame, which was only a few decades ago. This new stage was just that of a teenager given leeway from his or her parents: Rebellion.

"Niggas never really seen paper in this world
American blacks the teenagers of this world." ³

• Nas •

Blacks not only wanted to control their own destiny—they wanted to redefine it. Previously, we were being used as simple pawns in the chess game of movie making; however, persons and organizations took it upon themselves to counteract the deliberate efforts of Hollywood and produce works they knew to be genuine and sometimes hyperbolic representations of their culture. Whether it was Gordon Parks or Melvin Van Peebles, they responded with their own first-hand interpretations of black life. Organizationally, the NAACP was a strong advocate for the diversity and need for blacks to control the images that represent them, stating that:

"We will not tolerate the continued warping of our black children's minds, violence and cultural lies that are pervasive in current productions of so called black movies . . . The black community should deal with this problem by whatever means necessary." [4]

Negro Americans, for obvious reasons, were never granted the opportunity to make something of ourselves and we were dismissed as mentally inferior, lazy, and downright unfit to sustain our own independence. Regardless of the illogicality of our history, it is a part of our story, and because of the oppressive nature of our country at that time, Negros suffered to make a name for themselves on and off screen.

Think about it. Negros were considered to be childlike, mostly due to the slave culture along with black and white film and television stars that depicted us as such. In some aspects of this argument, I would have to agree. In Frederick Douglass' *The Narrative of Frederick Douglass*, he describes an adult male slave who contemplated leaving his plantation to find a better life up north, yet the plantation was all he knew, and he would have been lost as soon as he left his "home"—just like a child. Also, when basic liberties such as reading and writing are prohibited, one cannot be properly educated and therefore, his or her brain cannot grow; they cannot learn about cultures, politics, history, math, science, the arts—anything! When you consider at that time the childlike mental makeup of a slave—not because of their ineptitude to learn, but because they were denied the opportunity—the long lasting effects of slavery become apparent in the following generations.

So being children, once slaves were freed, some sought to do the unfamiliar and acting was something that they had not experienced before. Unfortunately, that world was ran by a system motivated by the very prejudices they had just left. After the days of Stepin Fetchit, Bill "Bojangles" Robinson, and Hattie McDaniel and the beatings, hosing, hangings, bombings and burnings, black people decided to deliver a message that went against the popular assumptions and commercial nature of the mid-20th century minstrel era. In that sense, blacks were teenagers of their time; just like a teenager's popular rebellion phase, we too, were eager to rebel against the system of traditional authority and blaze our own trails through innovative and demonstrative motion pictures.

After being deprived of creative liberation, Blaxploitation films condemned "The Man" for his relentless barraging of their films and exploited caricatures. This era would redefine black actors all together, movies such as *The Black Klansmen* (1966), which was catalytic in depicting a black man out for revenge against the KKK whom had killed his daughter, this type of retaliation was a foreshadow of the genre's perspective of whites in authority and whites in general. Also, *If He Hollers, Let Him Go* (1968), while rated very low amongst critics, was another film which helped to broaden the landscape of blaxploitation films, featuring a black character who was a wrongfully accused fugitive of the law; the film also included taboo sex scenes. The movie *Slaves* (1969) may be placed in the same thematic regard, illustrating blacks had decided they would run away from their oppressor and find liberation—by any means necessary. The movie *Cotton Comes to Harlem* (1970) was also important for a number of reasons; not only was this film directed by Ossie Davis, but it demonstrated how blacks were capable of running and operating successful businesses on their own. *Cotton* also indicated we were capable of being fooled by our own people through violence, lies, and manipulation; it served as a reminder separate from the other films which solely depicted whites as the only evil entity threatening blacks. *Cotton* showed the audience that blacks can be just as cunning as whites, if not more. The movie was also one of the first black action movies which offered some of the best "jive talk" of the era, gunplay, black protests, and references of "whitey" as a generalized caricature. *Cotton* was also one of the more successful releases in this era, proving there was, and still is, a market for blacks on screen without a top hat or serving as "The Help."

Other notable films such as *Super Fly* (1972), *Cleopatra Jones* (1973), *The Mack* (1973), *Blackenstein* (1973), *Three Tough Guys* (1974), *Willie Dynamite* (1974), *Five On The Black Hand Side* (1973), *The Black Godfather* (1974) and over 200 such films were released from 1960-1980. With the high volume of Blaxploitation films being released, it is easy to see how that particular era's most recurring motifs are still apparent in our contemporary culture. Figures such as Magic Don Juan, Flavor Flav, Snoop Dogg, Lil Jon, and other young African American men have modified their language and worn flamboyant zoot suits of the 70s. Consequently, many young black men referred to themselves as "pimps" soon after that period of time when black was bold, ubiquitous, and unapologetic.

On street corners across America, you will find employees, also known as "hoes," who do all the work and give their employers or "pimps" the profit of their labor. You see, there is a commercial force which exists behind stereotypes with hints of realism. Some individuals profit from the stereotypes and depictions on-screen and exaggerate the associating characteristics in order to set the new trend. Nonetheless, there is also a consumer who is watching them and taking notes on how to become the image they see. For instance, in *New Jack City*, we see Nino Brown's compound is protected by rottweilers, and shortly thereafter, drug dealers began using rottweilers, pit bulls, and other "aggressive breeds" in order to protect their illegal profits.

Whether it is Diddy's association with Ciroc which speaks to a luxurious and celebrated lifestyle or another product that caters to a specific market, celebrities are constantly influencing culture in one way or another. Let us not forget how Jay-Z's boycott of Cristal champagne in place of Armand de Brignac (Ace of Spade) compelled consumers to change their buying habits and preferences overnight. We are talking about several hundred dollar bottles of champagne which were used to influence buyer behavior and represent a symbol of empowered economic status, so just imagine the amount of free influence which powerful and polarizing persons can have on the personalities and sensibilities of a culture. When someone can alter another person's behavior based upon his/her recommendations, then the viewer becomes vulnerable and susceptible to whatever the purveyor is presenting now and later. As we have learned over time, once a company or person has established a market or basis for who will love and adore them, regardless of their discrepancies, that in turn gives the purveyor of that market the authority and clearance to do or say whatever he or she pleases without second-guessing or challenging the message being directly presented to the avid consumers.

The consumers not only look to the movies for entertainment and buying habits but for guidance as well. When one reflects upon how many young black men, in particular, come from single-parent homes, it becomes obvious why movies can have influence over their peers or parents. A role model is likely seldom to be seen in those surroundings, and it is because of that absence, which usually creates disdain or ambivalence, that any imagery of another celebrated black male becomes hyper-romanticized. Suddenly the character on-screen is something to be revered, regardless of his role—just seeing someone "make it big" is enough to inspire those onlookers to pursue a life akin to that character.

Symbolism, through entertainment and sports, has always—at least in my lifetime—been seen as an attainable, and frankly, easier pathway to success than the political, scholastic, business, healthcare, scientific, and conventional methods of what our country defines as a successful career. It is a dilemma which is often mentioned in various circles, and I have found myself puzzled by the reaction of some people to it. When you consider how a vast majority of athletes and celebrities did not come from an established pool of wealth and actually had to work their way up from nothing, they had to look at their surroundings and make a judgment call about what they wanted to do and who they would follow.

". . . The attitude of the imprisoned group may take three main forms,—a feeling of revolt and revenge; an attempt to adjust all thought and action to the will of the greater group; or, finally, a determined effort at self-realization and self-development despite environing opinion." [5]

• W.E.B. Dubois, 1903 •

As I have mentioned, when one wants to move up in his or her field or pursue their passion to its fullest potential, decisions are made to either do what they know to be true or produce a second hand and often fabricated or exaggerated depiction of what they have actually lived. The quote above speaks to the imprisoned, in this case not of literal incarceration but more so in regards to the captivity of creative expression. If one cannot immediately enter the field and turn it on its ears, the three options provided above are a realistic observation of what we have viewed in films within the last hundred years. One option, "to revolt and revenge," would best describe Spike Lee's abrupt arrival and longevity in Hollywood. The second, "to adjust all thought and action to the will of the greater group" would reflect Perry's work thus far. Lastly, the third option of "self-realization and self-development" is what most artists struggle with as they attempt to thrive in an industry which typically restricts creative thought and action. It is a dilemma with which many people in the entertainment industry have to contend: Is rebelling against the system the best way to stand out amongst the crowd? Or would it be more substantial to adjust to the norms of that very established commodity? Perhaps what is best is to self-evaluate one's own talents and draw from that? Whatever conclusion an individual resolves for themselves, they have decided to employ a thought-process which will lead them throughout their career. This is not exclusive only to directors; actors too have found themselves embroiled in this conundrum.

For blacks in particular, it seems even within our own culture, there is a sense of judgment which is rarely seen by other ethnicities. In 2011, for example, Boxer Bernard Hopkins effectively called NFL Quarterback Donovan McNabb an "Uncle Tom" for his passive and accommodating demeanor throughout his career. Hopkins also compared McNabb to a "house nigger" who does his job, does not ask much of his master, and causes no uproar in fear of agitating his superior. This insult is of the highest degree amongst black men in the U.S. because it essentially questions one's heart against a system which has historically taken advantage of people who look like you and infers that your disposition is a complacent and inferior one. For one black man to accuse another of not only being accepting of the system, but cheerfully complying with it is an insult unmatched by any other.

While both men are from Philadelphia, PA, Hopkins has always been a more brass and confrontational persona than McNabb. During McNabb's career, he was known as someone to let things work themselves out, never really complain, and keep his mouth shut when reporters ask him for comment about a number of different controversies. McNabb has always responded as an apologist with a nonchalant attitude towards the system that had taken advantage of him over and over. Just as "house niggers" would tell their masters of the "field niggers'" intentions of running away, reading and writing by conceiving themselves as privileged and more attractive than their usually darker counterparts—this caused a rift between slaves that is still evident amongst some black people today. Field niggers were believed to be more bold and less tolerable of their master's beatings and wrongdoings and would often run away, attempt to become literate, and unite with other slaves far beyond the master's approval. The hard, back-breaking work they performed was just one reason they hated the house niggers. While they were tending to the master's field, the house niggers often lived inside the "Big House," a term for the master's home. A house nigger ate his food and performed far less physically demanding work than they did. Field slaves saw this separation as an advantage to the house slaves—not understanding the sexual, mental, and physical torment house slaves often encountered by the master and his family. Additionally, the female house slaves often endured, not only unwanted sexual advances from her "master," but also the envy and mistreatment of the master's wife. These differences in lifestyle caused a derisive view of each other that, regardless of its logicality, is continually categorized within the "Uncle Tom" or "Nat Turner" characterization.

Most black men would identify with the sentiments of Bernard Hopkins as an awareness of one's place in this world becomes increasingly evident with age. There are certain behaviors, attitudes, demeanors, and conversations that you become aware of as you age which are relevant to you and your race. For a black man in America, it is the watered-down juxtaposition of joining the aforementioned Malcolm X or Martin Luther King, Jr. fighting for civil rights; while both essentially wanted the same thing, they had two different ways of getting it. Just as Booker T. Washington and W.E.B. DuBois had done over a century ago in addressing integration, all of these men had similar goals; however, it is apparent that some were willing to wait while others had urgent demands and refused to appease their white counterparts by accepting their draconian treatment as normal.

In my personal experiences, most black men pride themselves on being able to think freely and create their own destinies—this is something which is still relatively new to us as a people. As the dirt under America's social ladder, we pride ourselves on making something from nothing—so little is expected from us so when we become successful, it makes it that much more gratifying. That is where characters in these particular movies, especially O-Dog of *Menace II Society*, come from. O-Dog shows he is so real, so official, so "black" that he does whatever he wants, without worry of the consequences. A "crazy nigga" with no regard for his future, or his present for that matter, has been so brainwashed by the lifestyle and expectations of what it means to be a black man that he resorts to actions far surpassing the language, actions, and lifestyle of his black cinematic predecessors.

No one can ever say a particular movie reaches every facet of African American life, yet, there are black films which serve a greater purpose to their people. The 90s saw a major trend of violence and revolt, not only fictionally but also in real life, which made it necessary for directors to elaborate on the victims' lives so audiences can understand the life story and purpose the evening news and national media overlooks or considers to be just another homicide or arrest. This imbalance of power has been documented for years, even before slavery, where white men often dominated black men through authority, power, and lifestyle, which is to some degree, still apparent today.

These tensions and frustrations have been mounting over the course of over four decades, and the slightest misstep could set off a riotous and rebellious people. That is what the cheap and malicious beating of Rodney King and the subsequent riots and protests represented. What other reaction would you expect from a people who had nothing else to lose and saw the results of their idle watch? These movies speak to the segment of a nation who understand black people are not just some ravenous and dangerous group, but that their environment and socioeconomic status has dictated their reactions, and while the viewer may not agree with all of their decisions, they do understand *why* they chose that path.

As I mentioned earlier, to create an image, persona, or character that is to be emblematic of African American lifestyle is nearly impossible and often comes off as a disrespectable attempt to generalize us in a never-ending negative connotation. Stereotypes solely exist to encourage us not to think of individuals as individuals, but rather as members of a larger group with associated oversimplified expectations. One would be hard-pressed to find any other industry than entertainment in which stereotypes are used to the benefit of those producing the artists, actors, dancers, etc. Many of the characters we see today are the product of those very stereotypes depicted years ago. If it had not been for Sidney Poitier, can we truthfully say anyone would know or care who Denzel Washington is? It is because of the exploitations and malnourishment of quality screen characters that we can celebrate the fact that there is a black man who is one of the top earning writers, producers, and directors of all time, such as Tyler Perry.

Going as far back as Shirley Temple and her favorite on-screen partner, Bill "Bojangles" Robinson, the black viewing audience has taken up issue with the depiction and message of the actors portrayed on screen. In his days, "Bojangles" was nothing more than comic relief, a man who was always smiling, dancing and never seemed to have a bad day with family issues, sickness, career decisions, or heaven forbid—racial or societal opinions. Nope, "Bojangles" tap danced and went about his way, out of the camera frame to let a white child continue to blossom, using an innocence and wit which mainstream America continued to eat up. However, the point has been made before that "Bojangles" dumbed himself down to a child-like manner as well, once again resembling the old "Toms" who did whatever was asked of them without question and danced merrily to the master's pleasure. Though "Bojangles" was seen as something of a partner to Shirley Temple, it was clear he followed her lead, whether through dance or adolescent conversation. This stereotype would live, and in some instances, continue to permeate our popular culture with the belief that blacks are dancers with no intellectual capacities beyond that. His contemporaries such as Mantan Moreland would carry this tradition on as well, using his bulging eyes and choreography to move his way up from nothing substantial to international notoriety. It is because of the success of these stereotypical caricatures that they have been reproduced many times since their inception and apparently will continue to be reproduced.

It seems to be a clear attempt to disguise the realities of what a black man looks, talks, or acts like, regardless of the social progress or distress surrounding him. This was no more apparent than in the mid to late 1960s when riots were surfacing across the country and half of the United States was in ruins when blacks ravaged and rioted in the streets to receive the justice they were denied especially with the killing of Martin Luther King, Jr. Starting in Watts in 1965, there would be a consistent vociferous and unstoppable outrage in the form of rioting, looting, beatings and killings that would change the landscape of many parts of this country, even today. With blacks becoming increasingly more bold and unafraid of the consequences of expressing themselves in violent overtones, America was a combustible society at that time. It was the reality of the new and temporarily threatening presence of nationwide violence which made Sidney Poitier a truly fictional character in that day and time.

Many accused Poitier of not portraying the truest essence of what black America was going through during its most violent and uncertain period of civil unrest. It also did not help that Poitier was the most celebrated and prestigious actor of his time, as proven by his Oscar winning performance a few years earlier in the 1963 film *Lilies in the Field*. Poitier's films and characters did not represent what America at large was seeing on the nightly news, and more importantly, they did not identify with his seemingly accommodating and non-threatening depiction of a black man facing the white power structure. Poitier's roles never confronted race or provided an avenue to express the frustrations of people who looked like him when they felt they needed him most. A person of his stature and popularity at the time, in their minds, could have broken down barriers and opened a dialogue for race relations which may have advanced their cause even further. He was excoriated throughout his career for not taking the unpopular but well-known stance of his people, which in turn could have been detrimental to his film career. The same criticism, though not as harsh, was made of Bill Cosby with his comedic stand-up routine and later *The Cosby Show*, which some criticized for only depicting middle to upper class blacks and not highlighting the struggles of the population that had not aspired to the ranks of the Huxtables.

Poitier was also stripped of something too strikingly familiar with slavery, an aspect which was subdued and watered-down for film adaptation. His characters, as previously mentioned, were often absent of the on-screen romances or sexual temptations other movie stars were routinely given. During the days of slavery, in some instances, male runaways who were captured would be brought back and castrated in front of everyone not only as an example to them to not run away, but to literally cut off what fundamentally makes him a man, just like the Madea characterization today symbolizes. Hollywood essentially did the same thing to Poitier by removing any semblance of love, passion, or lust that would make him human in the least bit. In an article by black writer Clifford Mason in the November 1967 issue of *The New York Times* entitled, "Why Does White America Love Sidney Poitier So?" he calls Poitier "a showcase nigger" among other insulting attacks on his character as a person, not an actor. Mason predicts at his article's end Poitier will continue his career as a reassuring presence for white superiority as the "good nigger that he is." [6] Author, activist and commentator James Baldwin confronted this issue in a much more comprehensive context, blaming the very structure of America's fantastical expectation of blacks on screen, commenting, "If the black man's life were on that screen, it would destroy the fantasy totally." [7]

Professional Football legend turned activist and actor Jim Brown would prove to be the antithesis of Poitier's coy and reserved humility and serve to illustrate a hyper-sexualized and violent character the audience had been denied for some time. Brown would become so successful at his newfound acting career he could charge $150,000 a picture, a price at the time, which rivaled even the top paid white actors.

In my estimation, many critics of that time, and even now, have a contradictory stance on the issue of black actors in the media. On one hand they may state a coy and suppressed person such as Poitier is detrimental to the black man's image and he looks like a "Tom," accepting whatever laws and limits are given to him by his white master. On the other hand, if we have an actor such as Jim Brown who exhibits the very characteristics Poitier lacks, we then turn around and call Brown a "Buck" or "savage," hedonistically going through his life without much depth to his character but rather highlighting his sexual prowess and/or proneness to solve issues with a semi-automatic or revolver handgun.

Not to be too rhetorical, but how can one realistically watch a film starring black characters and not categorize them as neither a "Tom," "Buck," "Coon" or any other stereotypical image we have intrinsically learned to identify? An argument could be made for hardly any movie that a certain character is exhibiting the characteristics of a "Tom" if he agrees or follows the lead of a white man or woman. Was Denzel Washington representing a runaway or distrustful and manipulative slave in the 2011 movie *Safe House*? Was Samuel L. Jackson filling in as the "angry black man" in *Pulp Fiction* (1994) and nearly every other film he has been in? Well, that may not be fair. Nonetheless, the black actor is seemingly always scrutinized for accepting or performing roles which do not allow for the type of creative expression or flexibility their white counterparts are given.

The status of black people in America has been well-documented and is quite apparent. Since our "arrival" in this country, we have in large part been purposefully marginalized and subjected to poor wages, drug infestations, menial jobs, and provided a low standard of living, in terms of our majority. Socioeconomic status aside, I need not go over the many occurrences of how blacks have been flagrantly objectified from the literal sense of many years ago to the politicized efforts of marginalizing us today. Presently, African Americans are still largely under or unemployed, as represented by our unemployment rates doubling that of Caucasians. According to the Labor Department, the unemployment rate for blacks was at 14.4% in May of 2012, while the white unemployment rate was calculated at 7.4%. [9] These are not jobs as directors, actors, producers and the like. These are the jobs that pave the roads we drive on, build the fax machine we frantically send a resume to, and the battery we use in our cell phones to follow up with that employer. These are the jobs people are fighting for, nothing extravagant—just a job where one can earn a decent wage in which to support themselves and their family.

Inaccurate perceptions are the reason for these disparities; ideas that we have about one another continually contribute to the demise of the black middle and lower class. It is often those same classes which our most influential directors arose from. After living a life of disadvantage, once a black director is afforded an opportunity to make a film on a large scale, it is not only a dream come true, but there are certain pressures which go along with that privilege. When one considers the leaps and bounds a director must take in order to shine above his/her counterparts, it becomes obvious a choice is often made to reach that pinnacle of success.

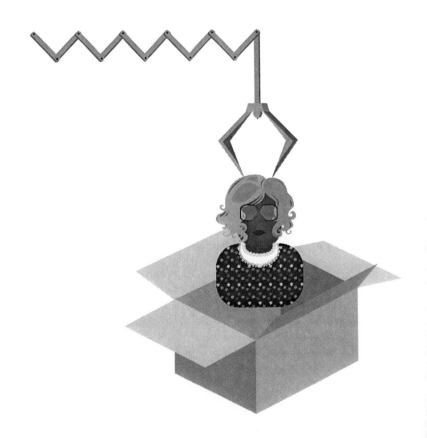

The Get Back

"Either they don't know, don't show, or don't care about what's going on in the hood." [1]

• Ice Cube as "Doughboy" •

The culture of the United States of America has been something of a changing landscape over the last century, more than any other century before it. To put this into perspective, in a matter of one hundred years, African Americans have visibly experienced oppression, segregation, civil discourse, hate crimes, salacious legislative battles over basic human rights, integration, pop culture identity re-configuration, drug epidemics, egregious incarceration rates and the commercially culminated achievement of a black President. When a country full of people have experienced some of the most heinous and degrading forms of dehumanization, it is apparent why progression and evolution are the last things one may see or hear from media outlets.

According to Paula J. Massood, author of *Black City Cinema*, a distinguishable variation in the themes between the Blaxploitation era and the 1990s boom of hood films was the purpose of the protagonist or the target of the storyline. After so many years of degradation, black people pointed to "the man" as the supreme evil and literally dismissed or eliminated him whenever he did or said anything opposed to the black character. However, according to Massood, the target shifts from the white oppressive establishment to persons in the same environment as the protagonist. The ghetto and its inhabitants became the new villain for street narratives and focal point for the most popular films of the 90s. [2] The shift is apparent in every major hood film, beginning with *Boyz N The Hood* which served as a real life interpretation of what was going on in the streets, as the unemployment rate for black youth in Los Angeles county was at a "staggering 45 percent through the late eighties." ³ Just as nearly all the characters in *Boyz N The Hood* and *Menace II Society* had no job or source of economic stability, almost half of their local viewing audience was in a similar predicament—demonstrating the very real adaptation of what it meant to be a black man in Los Angeles at that time.

Oct 25, 1990

This date symbolizes the very moment when things changed in African American culture, a date when all things conservative and traditional would be challenged to the core. On this day, a group of young black men would release an album that would set the world on fire with amazement and utter fear. This album would come to show the world, especially the authority figures in the world, that there was a segment of blacks who would not idly stand by as their friends and family were unfairly mistreated, abused, and sometimes killed. These "Niggaz Wit Attitude" released *Straight Outta Compton* and became famous among blacks and infamous among a large part of white America who feared what they may say or do next. This group embodied what conservative white middle–class God fearing Americans were afraid of most—young, black, and threatening youths with enough power and platform to exploit the racial injustices done to them with their equally volatile responses to an ever-present threat. NWA marked an "attitude" unheard of at that time and its response consisted of something no one could have imagined. The most dangerous thing about what NWA was saying is that their stories and tales of ghetto life, crack cocaine, gang banging, police brutality, and political corruption, were not merely things they whimsically talked about or transformed into a popular war cry in order to sell records, but these things were happening all around them and they were reporting to their audience, much like news reporters do.

It seems other forms of entertainment within the black community have flourished without exemption to those who came before them, art forms such as music have thrived off of personalities such as Kanye West, Lil Wayne, Nelly, Young Jeezy, Kendrick Lamar, and others who have profited from hip hop's diversity and embracement of different cultures, perspectives, stories and styles. Music, which was predominantly a white dominated industry from the business and profits standpoint, was conservative by design and blacks had to conform to what a white man's vision typically was. It was not until the emergence of music legends such as James Brown or Lionel Richie that blacks began to see they could create and maintain their own style of music and profit from it themselves. This is something I would have expected to see from the film industry by now, an emergence of directors, screenwriters, and producers who create a differing perspective of black film whom are not to be categorized as "toms," "mammies," or hedonistically ignorant; all the same, we are still awaiting this breakthrough.

Think about the similarities between film and music. They both have a perpetuated message and a theme to keep the viewer or listener hooked from the first scene or track until the last. Even with the emergence of *Boyz N The Hood*, it was because of NWA's lyrical challenge of the status quo which caused one of the biggest ruffles in conservative American society. Though Singleton's *Boyz N The Hood* was semi-autobiographical and visually drew in an audience which could see the rise and fall of a relatable character like Ricky, it did not have the impact of what NWA did—and that is only referring to one album. Admittedly, most of the media across the country initially denied them access to radio and television; nevertheless, once the demands of their street fame outgrew Compton, outlets such as MTV had no choice but to acknowledge them as an emerging group with a potent message that needed to be heard not only for social consciousness or to gain awareness but to draw a profit and increase ratings, much like when MTV finally decided to play Michael Jackson's videos earlier in the 80s.

The streets of Compton, California were flooded with crooked cops, drugs, dealers, and people who perpetuated the status quo—with the NWA putting these issues to the forefront of America through music their people could relate to, it catapulted them into a stratosphere most other groups have since failed to reach. Major record labels and syndicated radio stations across the country were so afraid of NWA and their hardcore lyrics they never gave them the time of day and simply wrote the group off as hoodlums and second-rate gangsters. It was not until their street credibility and buzz expanded out of Compton that national media outlets were forced to play their music and embrace them as musical revolutionaries.

That particular moment proved there was a major segment of our country America was unaware of, and it is because of Dr. Dre, Ice Cube, Eazy E, MC Ren, and DJ Yella that we were exposed to some of the most controversially accurate and disturbing music ever heard. Even though the group would eventually break up, their message is considered legendary not only in rap music, but American society.

To prove the pervasiveness of their group, one need not look at their record sales, cross-cultural appeal, or fruition of future events— one only has to note how the Federal Bureau of Investigation (FBI) was sent after them in order to discourage the group from producing anymore music that would "encourage violence" against police and authority figures. The FBI, or more specifically, a division called COINTELPRO, Counter Intelligence Program, had a similar interest in the causes of Fred Hampton, Malcolm X, the Black Panther Party and other "militant" blacks in the 1960s. To see that very governmental agency is still alive, well, at keeping any black man with a powerful voice censored—if not eliminated—is appalling. At the time, it was a badge of honor the NWA wore proudly as they continued to make the hits that provided a canvas for *Boyz N The Hood*.

July 12, 1991

This is the date that would spawn an entire decade of films looking to surpass its relentless brutality, ghetto introspection, street theme, and sheer authenticity. On this date, more than twenty years ago, *Boyz N The Hood* was released and ever since then, directors have used its model to bring forth the next wave of critically acclaimed hood films which filmmaker John Singleton was able to capture. According to some critics, the themes may have been exaggerated to fit into a stereotype of young black males living in the hood. In doing so, it also changed the way our country looked at young black men and in some aspects, how we looked at each other.

For years, we all knew violence, drugs and prostitution were synonymous with impoverished areas of America; however, it had never been expressed with such care for the individuals involved in those circumstances who would otherwise be seen as just another black male killed in an alley, instead of a college bound star running-back like Ricky. We knew their stories; we understood their struggle, their trap, for 107 minutes we were invested in their lives—for better or worse. The movie offered relatable figures, individuals whom we can say we see in ourselves or someone else. For instance, there is Doughboy, who lives day-to-day without thinking about what he is doing and has no foreseeable plan for his future. Being an ex-convict, there is limited upward mobility so he often finds himself stuck between the resentment of his brother Ricky and 40 ounces of liquid relief. There are persons like this is in nearly every circle, someone who feels they have been slighted and instead of rebounding or trying to find an alternate way to success, they merely talk about their problems without mentioning a possible solution. His brother, Ricky, is making the type of progress ghetto dreams are made of. Even though he had a child before graduating from high school, Ricky's football talents are sure to take him further than anyone in their hood has ever been. Ricky was the very symbol of one of Notorious B.I.G.'s legendary bars of "Either you slinging crack rock or you gotta wicked jump shot" when considering of possibilities of how to best escape the hood, two paths that many young black males continue to choose between today. [4]

Ricky is the star athlete of his hood; since a young age, he played football and stuck with it throughout his formative years. Between Ricky and Doughboy, Ricky is the child who can do no wrong in the eyes of their single mother, who is so proud of him and equally disgusted by her other loafing son, reminding her of their father who never makes an appearance on screen. While Ricky and Doughboy have their moments of contention like brothers do, it is not until Ricky's murder that Doughboy shows love in the only way he knows how: retaliation through the same violence that killed his brother.

Caught in the middle of all of this is their mutual friend Tre', whose father and mother are separated. Both parents want the best for their son, not through empty promises but through action. Tre's mother is earning her Master's Degree and his father is instilling in Tre' life lessons which represent the educated, family-oriented, and conscientious elements of black America. Moreover, it also serves as a reminder to African Americans that just because parents are not together does not mean they cannot be cordial and do what is best for their child. In the midst of the madness this movie presented, it always reeled the audience back in to what was important; it was imperative for Singleton to highlight a character like Tre' so there would be a balance of perspectives, as opposed to one absolute ideology which overpowers the viewer's ability to choose whom they identify with most.

You see, for young black men in America, though we may not be able to relate to Doughboy's incessant aggression, Tre's storytelling, or Ricky's athleticism, we likely could relate someone to them, whether by firsthand account or secondary observation. These characters became ingrained in our psyches as models of black masculinity; not necessarily as something to emulate, but to recognize in our culture. Many of us come from single parent households, grew up in poverty, sold drugs, witnessed crimes, or felt like no one cared. It is because of these very different accounts that we are not only descendants of kings and slaves, but of leaders and slackers who have given us varying perspectives of what it means to be black in America.

Unlike the majority of the 90s black films, which were quickly dismissed as excessively violent and simplistic in their storyline, *Boyz* crossed borders no other film had done in its release. Although it was marred with gang-related violence in its premiere, just as *New Jack City* had been earlier in the year with two persons killed and thirty wounded, this could not besmirch the importance of the film's message and germane iconography. The film was so instrumental, particularly for California residents, the former Governor of California, Pete Wilson, recommended all citizens go see the movie. [4] In a world that has politicized the chicken sandwich, as seen in 2012 by

Chic-Fil-A's President Dan Cathy when he announced his company does not support same-sex marriage, it is hard to imagine a Governor advocating a film today that would be met with more vociferous and blind protest from people who are afraid to speak to their children about the realities of ghetto life in America.

Also, the foreshadow *Boyz N The Hood* provided our nation with is something that has to be recognized. In one particular scene, Ricky and Tre' are pulled over and harassed by a black police officer, who goes as far as pulling a gun out on Tre' just to prove a worthless point. This incident shows the self-hatred within our own culture as a byproduct of white's disdain for us. It is also because of this film the Rodney King beating of March 3, 1991 did not seem like such an aberration of police brutality in America, but more so just the status quo. Beatings such as these were rumored yet rarely documented; however, this brazen attack on a defenseless black man by white "authority figures" was something that sparked riots throughout the city of Los Angeles. This became a pivotal moment in African American history; it represents a time when the system was challenged not by non-violence but by violence. This time represents how we would no longer tolerate the blatant abuse and arrogance of a police and judicial system which has historically shown unwarranted aggression and hostility towards blacks. It is also a telling sign that we, as black men, are targeted—and have been for some time now—as not only socially distrusted persons but as menaces to society.

It took a film such as *Menace II Society*, directed by the Hughes

Brothers, Allen and Alfred, to illustrate the unabashed hatred and overt prejudice police had for blacks at that particular time. This is not to say police in general have a prejudiced view of blacks in America; however, there is a segment of the population that is still under the spell of white authority and black inferiority. This was shown most evidently by the blatant abuse and plotting of white police officers to sabotage the two main characters, Caine and O-Dog.

Menace's introduction takes the time to show the 1960s Watt's riots to present day including the repeated brutality that scarred the faces, soaked the clothes, burned the skin, and blackened the eyes of a people who were already "too dark." This recurring theme of black consciousness, even though the movies may have been ratcheted-up for entertainment purposes, gave the stories merit and credibility. It was imperative for directors to illustrate how blacks were not viscerally violent, but because of the history of inferiority that was enforced, revolt and violence were the most conscious decisions those young men could forcefully impose for themselves.

This film continued the aesthetical depiction of young black males who were rebelling without a cause or fear of any consequences. Much like Doughboy in *Boyz N The Hood*, the character O-Dog carries the title of the "unpredictable nigger," the one no one can trust or have any idea of what his intentions are. His violent rage cannot be subdued by his friend Shareef, who like many blacks, lived life on the streets and later proselytizes himself into the teachings and philosophies of Islam. However, Shareef's message of positivity and self-determination for blacks amidst the fast life of hedonism and hood ethics is constantly overshadowed and shunned by O-Dog and Caine. Shareef's diatribes do, however, shed light on the many black men who have positively influenced their communities through examples of brotherhood, responsibility, faith, and cultural pride. Nevertheless, it also shows that the message, though pervasive in some circles, falls upon deaf ears to those who have no willingness to change and look no further than the present to make decisions about their future.

As I have mentioned, the Blaxploitation era was significantly different than the 90s in various ways, yet one signifying tie was the music industry and the soundtrack's unmistakable addition to a film's storyline. From Curtis Mayfield's "Pusherman" in *Super Fly* to the introductory theme song for *New Jack City*, "For the Love of Money," these artists and directors can relate to the messages being broadcasted to the nation, as they have first-hand experiences and recognition of the ghetto to illustrate the effects poverty, politics, crime, and drugs can have on a community. No movie exploited these realities more than *New Jack City*.

As real and unedited as 90s hood films were, they simply did not deliver the utter violence, hood politics, community decline, and overt drug usage *New Jack City* brought to audiences nationwide. *New Jack City* displayed the rawest view of the ghetto inside the perspective of its users, its boss, and those in charge of bringing that operation to an end.

From the perspective of Nino Brown, the drug kingpin, the profits of a drug enterprise such as The Carter Projects provide an example of black prosperity and benevolence; he is able to give back to the very community he is robbing of a chance at normalcy and stability. Nino Brown is symbolic because he represents a major problem within African American culture; selling our people the very poison passed down to us through a nefarious outside source and aggressively contributing to the decline of our community and people. When there are so little visible black leaders in the public eye—especially in the hood—any option therefore becomes attractive. Nino Brown's clothes, style, women, and reputation gave him the appeal a variation of African American audiences could admire. However, it was the audience's motivations and ability to discern fact from fiction which ultimately determined how that movie was interpreted. Many of us chose to view it as entertainment, while others saw it as a feasible opportunity to make a comfortable living. That is what makes this movie more impactful than those mentioned before; it blurred the lines between where entertainment ends and reality begins.

New Jack City showed the inside operations of a drug empire, from the distribution of the drugs to the guard dogs in their haven for added protection. This film set precedents that are still followed today, in not only movies, but in real life examples like Lil Wayne's *The Carter* album series. *New Jack City* was not *Boyz N The Hood*, *Menace II Society*, *Dead Presidents*, *South Central*, or *Juice*—this organization was run by persons in appointed positions, the boss wore a suit to work, they handed out turkey on Thanksgiving, kept records of business activity, and most importantly, they employed and serviced members of their own community.

The perspective of the users of crack cocaine is captured through Pookie, played by Chris Rock, who shows the ups and downs of trying to kick a habit at the height of the crack era. Pookie exemplifies that no matter how hard someone tries, their addiction can overpower the potential they once had. In a very humanizing scene, Pookie yells at a female in a dispute over a crack rock, while she tells him she was once prom queen, and he responds, "You used to be a prom queen, now you aint nothin' but a prom fiend." This scene demonstrates to the audience how everyone who was on crack was not just someone addicted to drugs but rather these were people with real lives, real futures, and real promise.

What further sets *New Jack City* apart from the rest is its ability to make the viewer choose a side. On one hand, you have a drug dealer who is making a lot of money, and though he is killing his customers and essentially destroying their community, he lives a very lavish lifestyle full of every vice a man could want and answers to absolutely no one. On the other hand, you witness the people he has destroyed, relationships he has thrown away, an entire neighborhood he has exploited, and the paranoia which comes along with that particular lifestyle. This movie delivers some of the most memorable and unforgiving quotes, violence, "business practices," and philosophies still practiced today. It is for that reason I do not agree with this quote, yet I can see how

Keenen Ivory Wayans may have reached such a conclusion:

"The reason that we have a fear of Black people in America is not based on a film, it's based on the fact that every time you watch the news that Black face is associated with something heinous. Every time you see a murder, that's the face you see, every time you see a robbery, that's the face you see, every time you see a rape, that's the face you see. That's why you lock your door when I walk past your window, not because you saw me in a movie." [5]

• Keenen Ivory Wayans •

Lastly, the police, who are in charge of uncovering the scandal of Nino Brown's operation, give us an inside look at what the news often chooses to report. The undercover operation and infiltration of The Carter Projects was something most movie goers expected at some point in film. It was also the personal vendetta of detective Scotty Appleton, whose mother was killed by Nino Brown earlier in his life, which drove him to see to Nino's demise. It was because of this hurt and hatred, he decides to stalk Brown until his eventual murder, an ending like many of the main characters of this time period in film.

The business of making movies is something often left unmentioned in the creation of films, that is, until a film is lacking the necessary finances to be completed. This is the case in many black movies. Another case can be documented as recently as 2012, when *Red Tails* was released, a story about the segregation and discrimination the Tuskegee Airmen endured during their time in the mid-20th century Air Force. Though the film featured plenty of action sequences, storylines, and comic relief, it was still in jeopardy of never being released due to its central theme and accurate depiction of blacks as conquerors and masters of their own destiny, regardless of the systemic discrimination designed to handicap their abilities. This film, produced by *Star Wars* creator George Lucas, who has earned over an estimated 1.7 billion dollars, and is considered by many to be a visionary of past and present science fiction films, still had problems getting the funding he otherwise would have had if not for the movie's message. [6] This is similar to when Spike Lee needed the financial support from the likes of Oprah, Michael Jordan, Bill Cosby, and others to complete the production of *Malcolm X* in 1992 because Warner Bros. did not want to fully fund the film, thinking it would not yield an adequate return for their investment.

Limited funding for black films is nothing new to those in the industry; even the aforementioned *New Jack City* was produced for only $8.7 million and reached a gross profit of over $47 million, proving a film does not need the biggest budget or marketing scheme to be remarkably profitable. [7]

Though the 90s hood films were often a controversial and violent depiction of African American life, their popularity would run its course and eventually they were parodied in the 1996 film *Don't Be a Menace to*

South Central While Drinking Your Juice in the Hood. This comedy mimics memorable scenes of what was deemed as one of the most violent and endangering times in cinematic history. Enough time passed so the industry and its audience could look in the mirror and put an end to the genre which brought the realest and rawest form of sex, drugs, money, and guns to the silver screen.

This is not to suggest that films such as *Boomerang* (1992), *Jason's Lyric* (1994), *The Preacher's Wife* (1996), *Soul Food* (1997), *The Best Man* (1997) and others do not provide an alternative view of black people; however, the 90s largely represented a time when many of today's college graduates, young entrepreneurs, and mid to late twenty something's gathered their first taste of what life was like in the hood. Never have audiences approved of a genre's timelessness, message, and authenticity as it did at that point in recent history. The 90s used fictional characters to tell real stories of triumph, hard decisions, broken families, prosperity, and love and hate. It encapsulated the essence of where we were as a people; all with their own story to tell, something Perry has failed to do in many of his films presented thus far.

Using his pictures, Spike Lee has been able to translate different messages, themes, and tones like no other director has done before with the right amount of arrogance, elegance, artistic expression, and in-your-face demeanor, that his characters bring to the silver screen. A few years ago, there was a momentary quid pro quo between Spike Lee and Tyler Perry, two of the most successful and recognizable black directors in our nation's history. Since then, the two have made up and wished each other well.

While both men have contrasting styles of directing, producing, and acting, they share a common bond that has linked similar audiences consisting of individuals who were once overlooked and type-casted in a majority of films. The next two chapters will examine the two men's most profitable five films as an objective and balanced way of illustrating the titles which were more popular, not only as a result of content, but more importantly because of consumer preference and expectations.

After the influx of raw hip hop music in the 1990s which challenged the system at hand, rappers challenged each other, and ultimately challenged their listeners—this period made its successors conscious of what works and what ultimately does not work. At one time, there was a criterion one had to meet in order to be considered credible amongst their peers, critics, and listeners. They had to talk about issues of cultural importance and offer missing representations we as a people were not getting from the mainstream entertainment and media outlets. That hip hop renaissance period was most popularly influenced by artists such as KRS-One, Wu Tang Clan, A Tribe Called Quest, Ice Cube, Geto Boys, Public Enemy, Tupac Shakur and plenty of others who taught as well as entertained us. However, like all good things, that period came to an end and, as art imitates life, people became less interested in social issues and became more immersed in grandeur and commercialized messages of nothingness. The messages of yesteryear are far and few between, and certain artists, for their own reasons now, produce what is a watered down version of hip hop and black culture as a whole. Whether it is an accurate portrayal or not to most, it is indicative of where we are as a people.

There was a stream of black consciousness which began to surface in the late 1970s; it came from an arena that was unheard of on a national scale. Hip hop was proving to be the most pervasive and groundbreaking culture America had seen in years, and along with rappers, the cultural landscape of the South Bronx and New York was beginning to take shape—from graffiti, breaking (break dancing), deejaying, and emceeing—there was no substitute for the authenticity and style hip hop brought to the forefront. While some artists chose to highlight social problems in hopes of bringing attention to them, others indulged in the hedonistic components which a local or national celebrity had brought them. In either case, many people took notice of this rapidly evolving culture, none more than Spike Lee.

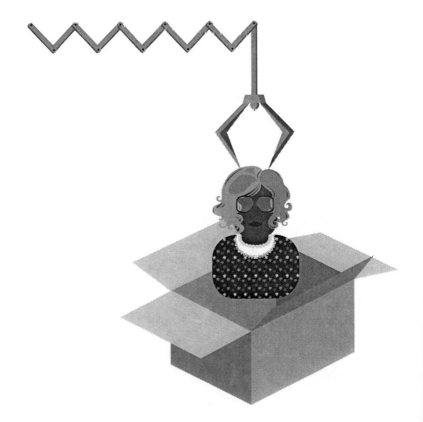

Last of a Dying Breed

". . . Blame it on the pigment" [1]

• Kanye West •

What Spike Lee has done for America cannot be under-valued or forgotten as his immediate presence and sustainability in the film industry is something that has yet to be duplicated since his arrival. More than merely iconic, his films and his "controversial" opinions are some things a large segment of blacks can relate to—a person who is intelligent, opinionated, and crass enough to speak his mind about a number of subjects which are meant to rub people the wrong way. Subjects like Huey P. Newton, Birmingham church bombings and Hurricane Katrina victims, etc. are all avenues a filmmaker searching for profits would easily deflect; on the other hand, Lee welcomes these stories of hardship, tragedy, and despair. Nevertheless, Lee has also created documentaries about Kobe Bryant and Michael Jackson, which show his range in pop culture and mainstream America as well. The quality of film and direction he is able to produce speaks volumes through these subjects as he often allows the story to tell itself and not be overshadowed by his presence and celebrity.

In many of his documentaries, Lee interviews persons in the story and allows them an opportunity to open up for the audience, giving them a full context of the person behind a particular tragedy. This is a specific talent of Lee's which is often absent in other documentaries; the ability to give the most affected persons a platform to tell their story without feeling like just another number in the big scheme of the media's exploitation of tragedy. In a typical documentary whether about a food epidemic, natural disaster, or corporate fraud, films usually spend the majority of the time looking at the problem on a macro level, presenting all-encompassing statistics, while never truly examining the people who are affected by the catastrophe.

Lee's documentaries can never be accused of taking the macro view, as he provides the viewer with gripping and unforgettable insight, exhibited in his 2006 documentary *When the Levees Broke: A Requiem in Four Acts*. One profile that particularly stands out is a black middle-aged man who, like so many others in New Orleans, had been displaced by the flooding and left his home with his elderly wheel-chair bound mother to go to the New Orleans Saints Super Dome for shelter and food. Throughout the chaos and mass hysteria, his mother was in need of water and shelter, as it was one of the hottest days in recent memory according to New Orleans residents. He attempted to retrieve some sort of aid for his mother as he knew she was feeling ill from the abrupt move from her home, and the smoldering heat was becoming more unbearable as the day went on. After running around frantically and unsuccessfully for his mother, he returns to find her dead in the wheel chair. If the story told by the son is not enough to put you in their environment to make it real, Lee ends the story with a picture taken by the mother's son of her slumped over in the wheel chair, deceased—evoking emotions of hurt, anger, compassion, and more hurt.

This is what makes Lee great; his ability to push the viewer's emotions to their breaking point, even when you believe you understand the context and emotional connections between the individuals and the event; he makes it as real and natural as only he can. It is this dedication to authenticity that has been a trademark of his characters on and off screen. It is also one of the reasons Lee was able to make such an incredible splash so early in his career with films like *Do the Right Thing, School Daze,* and *Jungle Fever.* In our generation, a black filmmaker had not made such pictures that spoke directly to a group of people in a manner of "us" rather than "them." Lee's characters in many of his films have a certain "je ne sais quoi" about them, you do not really know what it is, but there is something about the way they move, talk, and look, that the black viewer can relate to, either by firsthand account or someone we may know. Whether it is Greer in *She's Gotta Have It,* who is obviously more concerned with his own appearance than "Lola's," or the three old men always speaking their mind in *Do the Right Thing,* or perhaps the always Afrocentric and "militant" Dap in *School Daze*—these are all people the viewer can relate to because these people actually exist, and not only do they exist, they often resemble the characters in Lee's films.

It is a genuine feeling of relativism 27 year old director Ryan Coogler expressed in an interview when discussing *Fruitvale Station* (2013). When responding to a question regarding Oscar Grant's family being receptive to him producing a film about their deceased son, "...it also helped me being around the same age as Oscar, being from the Bay area, and having that perspective, not being somebody from the outside community..." This single picture from Coogler was a powerful and eye-opening experience moviegoers and film critics alike overwhelmed with praises and acclaim; however, this is also something Lee has done on a consistent basis for over three decades. Coogler recognizes the importance of authenticity in the work being produced, and he understood that by sharing the same skin, age, and location as the main character, he would be able to convey a more genuine and unfiltered message than a director unfamiliar with the culture and perspective of someone such as Oscar Grant.

> "Black members of the audience were beside themselves that a film was finally dealing with their lives, and in a manner that more closely resembled their sense of their own experience than the stereotypes being offered in Hollywood." [2]
>
> • Spike Lee •

As great as Lee has proven to be in creating his own destiny through the creativity of captivating his audiences, what is equally impressive is Lee's ability to financially profit from his films and to not conform to the expectations to which previous black entertainers have found themselves reduced. There have been numerous accounts of performers, musicians in particular, who have had illustrious careers and ended up broke in the end, much like many of today's professional athletes.

"What is always upsetting to me is when people do stuff and then they don't want the generation behind them to advance it. What we were able to do—we were able to make money. Some people have this idea that to be a true artist you have to be a starving artist, and I saw that from my father firsthand and that's not something that I wanted. I always felt that you can be an artist and still make money. Why should the record company, the movie studios, the owner of the sports team, the publisher, make all the money off your creativity? That doesn't make sense." [3]

• Spike Lee •

Lee also does a great job of not overexposing himself in his later pictures, which gives actors the chance to make their own marks as opposed to becoming a recurring and predictable caricature of himself. With such power and symbolism, I am sure the allure of delivering a message by not only directing, but being seen on camera, was tempting; in spite of that fact, Lee limited his roles in film by never making himself the protagonist of any one picture, but rather a supporting actor.

The versatility Lee has exhibited throughout his career is remarkable, considering other black directors who have not had the longevity and acclaim Lee has earned. From movies involving interracial dating, 20th century minstrel shows, drug dealers, black college life, a basketball prodigy, and every stereotype imaginable, Lee's movies reflect the world in which we live through a black scope that is often ignored and neglected by the mass media. However, in some instances, Lee directs something no one sees coming; such is the case for *Summer of Sam* (1999), *Inside Man* (2006), *Miracle at St. Anna* (2008), and *Oldboy* (2013)—he stepped outside of his comfort zone and received harsh criticism for some of those works as well.

One noticeable thing Lee does in many of his movies is provide the audience with scenarios where they have to pick a side in the story. Lee presents an in-depth social or personal dilemma, and it is left up to the viewer to take sides. He uses the power of conversation to accomplish this, such as in *Jungle Fever*, when females talk about the hardships of finding "a good black man" including miscegenation, down low brothers, infidelity issues, and inquiring if there is something that they, as black women, are not doing right. Never does one opinion get overshadowed by the other as Lee makes a conscious effort to let all points of view be freely and extensively expressed. This has become a staple of Lee's films, as he often gives the audience a scenario or a point of debate and leaves it for the public to digest and draw their own conclusions. Seldom does Lee present a social issue and give his opinion as the end all be all, but rather he meticulously gives every viable reasoning or option for the subject to be discussed and understood.

To say there is a shortage of cultural diversity in Hollywood directors would be a drastic understatement. The only consistent black filmmakers in the last twenty years to achieve worldwide fame and relative autonomy over their work are Tyler Perry and Spike Lee. It is no mistake this has occurred, as Hollywood has repeatedly denigrated the status of African Americans, from actors to directors. There are sprinkles of black directors here and there, yet when we speak of a consistent and credible black director, they are far and few between. In 2013, Lee used Kickstarter.com, a website where people can provide money to a worthy cause, in order to gain the necessary funding for an upcoming picture. However, before there was a Kickstarter, Lee worked tirelessly to gain funding by asking people in high positions for their financial assistance to help his pictures come to life. Using this example, Lee showed if something is so great and worthy of exposure to the masses, it is important to ask for the necessary funding from people who can provide it. This is a strategy actress Octavia Spencer, co-executive producer and actress of *Fruitvale Station*, also utilized in acquiring funding to finish shooting their film.

It is not difficult to understand why some may have been reluctant to financially support Lee's projects, as he often touches on subjects considered to be taboo. Lee's most controversial picture and highly anticipated film, *Malcolm X*, was released in 1992. Before Lee even began working on the film, poet, playwright, and activist Amiri Baraka commented, "We will not let Malcolm X's life be trashed to make middle-class Negroes sleep easier." This claim would not be ignored by Lee who would later respond saying, "Where's his book on Malcolm?" Lee also accused Baraka of not moving to Harlem until after Malcolm X had been assassinated. Lee, over the course of his career, has come to make friends and enemies because of his unfiltered, take-no-prisoners, by any means necessary approach to filmmaking and social politics. Lee, never allowing anyone to compromise his vision, continues to create works such as *Red Hook Summer* (2012), which was unpopular with both critics and viewers alike. Nonetheless, Lee does not allow the public to dictate his creativity and the motifs he confronts. He uses his experience to create films which sometimes speak to the masses, or in the case of *Red Hook Summer*, speak to a specific group of persons who have dealt with childhood molestation.

In this current generation, as I have learned, it is increasingly difficult to influence persons if their language is not being spoken or understood. What Lee did more than anything was fool people into dealing with each other. He bridged the gap between intellectuals and those who had not read a book in years. His films and content were real to the streets and they featured characters who dealt with real life issues. He also juxtaposed those issues with people who could confront them on an intellectual frame of thinking. Lee is able to merge two very different methodologies into one by presenting the culture as cool yet smart, a balance that is easier said than done. By creating "urban" films such as *Joe's BedStuy Barbershop: We Cut Heads* (1983), *She's Gotta Have It* (1986), *School Daze* (1988), and *Do The Right Thing* (1989) early in his directorial career, Lee made it comfortable for black people to see themselves on screen and feel comfortable with the director showing them in a certain light, as he speaks their language. Once Lee had established a target market with the black youth, he was able to branch out and create projects such as *Malcolm X* which Lee would have never been able to produce or release if he had tried this film in his earliest years. By establishing himself as a trustworthy and credible participant and purveyor of culture for Black America, it provided him with a license to create works that were not merely good movies but iconic films. With the style and sound of the youth resonating with most black movie goers, Lee had the reputation of someone who, though controversial, was also talented and directed quality pictures worthy of admiration from audiences near and far.

Lee has understood the importance of having balance in his audience for some time now; even in his 1988 film *School Daze*, he invited Rev. Jesse Jackson to bless the film and he did so by imploring the cast and crew to make a film of which no one could ever question the quality. Jackson also complimented Lee saying, "he represents a live alternative to misopportunity." [4] Lee understood the importance of having meaningful relationships with religious figures such as Jackson, mega celebrities such as Eddie Murphy, superstar athletes such as Michael Jordan, and common folks who would gladly support and contribute to the success of his films. As a result of having all of these different persons in his corner, it created a dependable and celebrity constituency most politicians could only dream to have. Spike Lee had the "Black vote." There was no demographic of blackness he did not speak to by the midpoint in his filmmaking career and audiences of all colors had taken notice. Best of all, this balance achieved by Lee did not come from a place where he felt like he was pretending to be something he was not.

> *"I've never run around trying to hide from my middle-class educated background, I've never tried to dumb down and say, 'I'm from the streets, the ghetto.' Why would I want to do that? I'm never going to devalue education, the educated background that I've come from or being educated myself. It's not a negative."* [5]

• Spike Lee •

Lee in fact, throughout his career, was supported by persons whom are synonymous with education, such as Dr. Henry Louis Gates Jr. who once stated, "he's the Jackie Robinson of the film community . . . I've been with Spike, people stop him in the street, they shake his hand, glad to know him, admire him." [6] The freedom to express himself gave Lee the opportunity to make films some people would see regardless of its content, merely because his name was attached to it. Conversely, he did not always enjoy the acclaim his earlier movies had earned him. Such as *Girl 6* (1996), which movie critic John Pierson, commented, "*Girl 6* is the only one of Spike's films that I think the world could live without." [7]

Not worried in the least about someone's opinion of his work, Lee's methods and messaging would undoubtedly rub some people the wrong way. He also has a tendency to push his own actors beyond their comfort levels. Most notably, in *School Daze*, between the light skinned "Wannabe's" and the dark skinned "Jigaboo's," Lee purposely created more dissension between the two groups of female actors. According to one actress, Lee put the light skinned women in a nicer hotel than the darker skinned females in hopes of increasing the amount of hostility that the women would display on screen. Joie, Spike's sister, had once commented she felt uncomfortable with her love scene in *Mo' Better Blues* (1990) with Denzel Washington, as her brother directed the film and the love scene.

In an attempt to document the most powerful films of Lee's career to this point, the five films featured are not to gauge what I believe to be Lee's greatest movies to date, but rather the films included are Lee's top grossing pictures which serve as an accurate measuring stick to what the public has deemed his best works and most valuable contribution to the world.

#1 Inside Man

A movie unlike most of Lee's prior releases, he directs a completely different and unexpected film. Lee works with Denzel Washington, with whom he also worked in *Mo Better Blues* (1990), *Malcolm X* (1992), and *He Got Game* (1998). In this particular film, Washington plays a detective who is inspecting an elaborate bank robbery and somehow finds himself on the wrong end of an FBI investigation. This movie, full of plot twists and tangles, uses a general and familiar theme of one of the oldest criminal acts in history; however, it is presented in a clever and sophisticated method by Lee.

This movie offers a different glimpse of Lee's talents and ability to think outside the box, both of which have already provided him with celebrity status, financial security, and international reverence. It is not only the capacity to produce a work no one is expecting, but it is also the quality of the work being presented. Lee, throughout much of his life had been categorized whether rightly or wrongly, as a socio-political activist and outspoken, culturally introspective lighting rod whose opinions were often thought to be off-limits. However, in *Inside Man*, there were no subliminal or blatant protests of a civil injustice or corrupt police official, as has been the case of many of Lee's pictures in the past.

This film had to be measured on its own merit as a quality picture; many people were amazed to find out Lee directed the film as it looked and sounded like nothing he had made before. The plot twists and development of characters provide for a storyline that left his audience guessing until the film's conclusion. When a director has made his name for so many years as an expert and authority figure on a particular genre or subject, the audience expects nothing but the best quality of his work in that particular field. When that director presents something unexpected and brilliant—it validates their earlier work and reintroduces them to a brand new segment of the population who otherwise may not know who they are. This would prove to be Lee's most financially profitable film to date; it is a work he can be proud of, not only for the commercial success of his picture but also because he did not have to compromise the integrity of his past works by presenting an oversimplified and intentionally bland movie solely targeted at profits.

#2 Malcolm X

In this provocative work, Lee offers his own perspective of the triumphs and tribulations of Malcolm X, with a detailed account of his story. Lee includes the important people in Malcolm's life and the religious affiliation which made him one of the most celebrated, and later, obscure orators and intellects of all time.

This particular film, to Lee's credit, was marketed beautifully to the public, regardless of their feelings and trepidations about Malcolm X. Lee made sure to promote the film with an aggressive promo tour where he even got Michael Jordan to wear an "X" baseball cap. Jordan's endorsement of the film simultaneously validated the film's significance and Lee as a credible director.

What is most telling of Lee's reign on top is that he was the most pervasive director on not only the silver screen, but the television screen. At a time when Michael Jordan's popularity was becoming ubiquitous throughout the world in the mid to late 80s, Lee associated himself with MJ through his shoe line and commercials which helped propel his name further than he could have ever done by himself. Michael

Jordan is arguably the most easily recognized athlete or celebrity in the world. With MJ's validation, Lee continued to make films that were anti-mainstream yet remained successful among his audiences.

Before its release, there was much apprehension by industry experts regarding how much an originally four hour film based on a controversial African American male would move the needle and make a profit. The film was also unjustly compared to the recent violent theater openings of that year's earlier *Boyz N The Hood* and *New Jack City*; Warner Bros. took note of the violent trends and made the decision to "open the film on Wednesday in order to lessen the possibility of guys with bad intentions having the public forum." [8] The studio also argued over the movie's length, which was later reduced to 3 hours and 22 minutes, complaining this would ultimately limit the amount of times film goers could possibly see the movie and produce a respectable profit. This theory backfired as *Malcolm X* would gross over $9 million opening weekend and north of $48 million in its lifetime sales, proving people would sell out theaters across the country to see a contentious and equally enlightening picture.

#3 Jungle Fever

This is a movie that would provoke discussion about interracial dating across the country. *Jungle Fever* sought to prove many of the stereotypes and beliefs that we, as Americans, had against one another to be nonsensical, funny, intimidating, and sometimes even deadly. Stereotypes involving black men and women and white men and women, were all on the table during the film. In a particular scene that speaks to the level of candor and authenticity of the script, a group of black women talk amongst themselves about their perspectives on black men, calling them "dogs, homos, drug addicts, or inmates." While this is a large part of the conversation, other women chime in refusing to believe all black men are bad or offer the perspective that love conquers all and no one group can be judged by the actions of a few. At the end of their conversation, the women mention the stereotypical aesthetics of a successful black man, and according to the women, in order for a black man to reach his highest peak, one needs to have a "white woman on their arms," a topic widely rumored in the African American community.

This conversation is emblematic of what *Jungle Fever* represents, a driving narrative of distrust, mixed in with some truth, and a few laughs provided by Samuel L. Jackson. The characters' dilemma and authenticity are always there to serve as a reminder that what you are watching is something that matters to your culture and its lessons are overdue yet tangible to the viewer. It showed that persons, regardless of socioeconomic status, had a certain perception of interracial dating, and regardless of their position in life, their judgments were usually based on ignorance, outdated stereotypes, and personal religious convictions.

If there is a piece of poetry I could use to equate what Jungle Fever means to me, it would be a poem entitled "To a White Girl" from Eldridge Cleaver in his groundbreaking autobiography *Soul on Ice* (1968):

I love you
Because you're white,
Not because you're charming
Or bright,
Your whiteness
Is a silky thread
Snaking through my thoughts
In redhot patterns
Of lust and desire

I hate you
Because you're white.
Your white meat
Is nightmare food.
White is
The skin of Evil.
You're my Moby Dick,
White Witch,
Symbol of the rope and hanging tree,
Of the burning cross.
Loving you thus
And hating you so,
My heart is torn in two.
Crucified. [9]

The first stanza describes the love and lustful pleasures a white woman's skin represents, which has nothing to do with her personality or charisma but only her body and his longing for it. The second stanza embodies the animosity and pain which her skin has caused over time with the symbolism of people who look like him being murdered for nothing but the color of their skin. Lastly, Cleaver, just like Flipper, finds himself torn between the lustful pleasures for this beautifully enigmatic woman and the historical consequences of acting upon this feeling.

#4 Original Kings of Comedy

In this unprecedented documentary/stand up special, Lee films four prominent African American comedians—Cedric The Entertainer, Steve Harvey, D.L. Hughley, and the late Bernie Mac at a showing in Charlotte, NC that would help boost the careers of each man who participated. While Lee did not control the content of the jokes, his influence was apparent in the method in which the movie was shot. Lee and his influence in this particular picture was instrumental in giving his audience a completely different side of his personality with an alternative perspective of African American culture which may have not translated as well through a traditional script.

With this film, Lee helped to open the door for all four comedians to expand their horizons and broadcast their talents to an entire nation that may have been unaware of them before. Lee also films them while off stage to showcase their true personalities and to get interviews from them while together, providing some of the most memorable quotes to this day.

The black comedian is someone who is revered in African American culture, from the legendary Richard Pryor or Dick Gregory who stood up for social change during the Civil Rights Era to the internationally renowned Chris Rock, and most recently Kevin Hart—black comedians have a way of relating to their audiences through shared experiences and *Original Kings of Comedy* encapsulated this very notion to perfection.

#5 Do the Right Thing

This film, more than any other of Lee's pictures, served as a reenactment to what was occurring in the streets of New York, and it reminded viewers of the present racism and violence which still exists today. Along with *Crookyln*, *Do the Right Thing* represents everything in Brooklyn Bed Stuy, according to Lee. This film provides the audience with a chance to immerse themselves in what it meant to be young, prideful, and culturally aware along with exactly what it meant to be black at that particular time. In fact, the film was so authentic, the graffiti art featured in the film "Tawanna told the Truth" was based on an actual 1987 alleged rape and abduction case where a young black woman testified six white men raped her and would later state she falsely testified against the men. It was believed by many people that external parties forced her to change her statement. In addition, Radio Raheem's killing in the film was inspired by the real life murder of a black graffiti artist named Michael Stewart who was choked to death. Blacks had also called for a boycott of a local Italian pizzeria at that time due to a senseless killing that had occurred in which a black man was killed for sitting in a pizzeria.

In the case of these instances, *Do The Right Thing* demonstrates how art was imitating life, and the film's characters and style represented an attitude of culture, love, contentment, protest, outrage, and death.

Heat is a constant factor in this film; throughout all of the ups and downs, changes of theme, laughter, heartache, anger and compassion—it is always hot and it creates an environment in which, just like the actors, the viewer cannot get too comfortable. The threat of violence is featured often in this film, whether it is from Pino and his brother fighting in the closet to the concluding mayhem that sets the neighborhood into a frenzy. The tone of this film is something that can truly be interpreted by the audience. One can remember such scenes as Radio Raheem's fluent explanation of love and hate, Sweet Dick Willie's jokes on his friends and the Korean shop, Tina's dance at the opening credits, or Buggin' Out's scuffed up Jordans that made this movie unlike anything the world had ever seen before. Lee exploits the idea of racism and how it can permeate an entire group of people to ultimately retaliate through violence while simultaneously gaining and losing a sense of cultural identity.

Films directed by Spike Lee

Rank	Title	Studio	Adjusted Gross	Release
1	Inside Man	Uni.	$112,837,800	3/24/06
2	Malcolm X	WB	$96,946,700	11/20/92
3	Jungle Fever	Uni.	$64,425,300	6/7/91
4	The Original Kings of Comedy	Par.	$59,151,400	8/18/00
5	Do the Right Thing	Uni.	$57,935,600	6/30/89
6	He Got Game	BV	$38,399,100	5/1/98
7	Mo' Better Blues	Uni.	$31,887,100	8/3/90
8	Summer of Sam	BV	$31,703,900	7/2/99
9	School Daze	Col.	$29,551,800	2/12/88
10	Crooklyn	Uni.	$27,253,100	5/13/94
11	Clockers	Uni.	$25,091,300	9/15/95
12	25th Hour	BV	$18,131,400	12/19/02
13	She's Gotta Have It	Isld	$16,064,200	8/8/86
14	Get on the Bus	Sony	$10,870,600	10/18/96
15	Girl 6	FoxS	$9,332,200	3/22/96
16	Miracle at St. Anna	BV	$9,209,600	9/26/08
17	Bamboozled	NL	$3,524,300	10/6/00
18	Oldboy (2013)	FD	$2,193,700	11/27/13
19	She Hate Me	SPC	$492,200	7/28/04
20	Red Hook Summer	Vari.	$363,200	8/10/12

Source: boxofficemojo.com Acquired: 2/18/2014

What separated Lee from past and present directors was his relentless appreciation and depiction of blacks in America, showing there is more than one type of black man—some are business execs, others are musicians, fathers, drug dealers, drug users, pedophiles, cops, ex-cons, basketball stars, revolutionary figures, and many more. Lee is not only introspective enough to look within his culture to point out the strides but he "keeps it real" and documents our shortcomings as well.

Lee also uses his introspection to tell a story that is relatable to the audience, not as a hyperbolic depiction of our people, but as accurate characters with stories many of us know. Lee also uses his talents to set the tone of filmmaking, showing that blacks do not have to be type-casted into the movie industry—that the days of stereotypical caricatures are long over and America at large, has moved on from that. It is something Lee uses much of in his movies; he uses racism to explain certain contexts within American society, and does so in the biggest cultural and ethnic melting pot in the world: New York. By understanding the undertones of racism on a social, political, judicial, and economic scale, it provides him with a large platform to express various perspectives of his culture.

Instead of pretending racism does not exist, Lee decides to confront the illogicality of racism toward each other, from not only blacks and whites, but blacks on blacks. Though he has a relatively small role in *School Daze*, the memorable scene of Samuel L. Jackson as a "local" talking to the Mission College students, is an example, as he tells them: *"I bet you niggas think yall white—college don't mean shit! Yall niggas and you gon' be niggas forever, just like us—niggas."* Jackson's character, Leeds, in typical Spike Lee fashion, addresses a serious issue by mixing in humor that only people who have had those types of conversations and contemplations can understand and appreciate. That scene speaks to the division, and sometimes resentment, existing between the formally uneducated blacks and those who have pursued a higher education. The uneducated assume that because someone chose to further edify themselves, they are "acting white;" this is the same stigma Senator Barack Obama addressed and effectively dismissed during his speech at the 2004 Democratic National Convention.

At a time when Lee was releasing movies at least once per year (1988-1992, 1994-2002), he remained the most controversial and polarizing figure in the movie industry by challenging taboo subjects many preferred not to talk about or draw their own conclusions without truly understanding the complexities and facing the realities of American culture altogether. Lee created works that could be appreciated years from their release, demonstrating the truest definition of a classic piece of art—whether we are talking about a Mozart painting, the Roman Coliseum, a Shakespearian monologue, or any other form of timeless admiration we have deemed classic. It is no less impressive how he was able to release his films with the amount of profanity, sexuality, and vitriolic themes that slapped a politically correct nation in the mouth.

There is another element to Lee's directorial talents; using African American documentaries to tell stories he felt needed more justification or an additional perspective to the portion of his audience who may be unaware of what is going on or has already happened. In his movies, racism always plays a part in the plot, whether it is for comic relief, or in some instances, to incite violence through words and/or actions. He uses it as a part of the story, yet racism rarely dictates where the story concludes. The characters are not as shallow to let a person's color define them and how they interact with others. Racism is used as casually as talking about the weather, and no incendiary topics are off limits. Whether it is Detective Klein's persistent and unprovoked obsession over finding a killer or Buggin Out's tiredness of seeing white people on the "Wall of Fame" at Sal's, the entire premise of *Jungle Fever*, or any of his other films; Lee never shied away from exposing exacerbating relationships between whites and blacks. Lee, a student of film and life, uses instances from our reality to create some of his films' most memorable topics and indelible imagery.

What made and continues to make Lee a polarizing figure in the filmmaking community is the respect he has earned over the last three decades. Without his contribution to film, there would be a large gap in the consciousness of black America. While always controversial and never apologetic, Lee has given the world a blueprint and exposure to their own culture and while some may not agree with his personality and unconventional tactics, it is unquestionable that Lee has bestowed a legacy anyone would be hard-pressed to emulate.

Chapter 6: Last of a Dying Breed

Black directors are often criticized unjustly, and when there are so many different populations, interests, and motivations, having a director represent an entire race of people can never fully satisfy all of their cinematic expectations. However, in terms of diversity, it would be inappropriate to accuse Lee of, if anything, being a complacent director and not demanding the most of himself and his actors. Lee, having been a director for over thirty years, has given America and people of color a sense of pride in filmmaking that may have not been there without him. Even though *Boyz N The Hood, Menace II Society, Coming to America, Harlem Nights,* and *The Wiz* are considered classics, those directors have not sustained an international interest and mainstream loyalty throughout their careers. He directed in a way which rivaled his predecessors, his style and persona proved to advance his career further than any black director before him. Nonetheless, if we look at the present, things have changed in a drastic way.

Most successful people had to make sacrifices in order to achieve their goals, from the school teacher to the lawyer to the doctor or the director. Actors are no different. Chris Rock, in his early days on *Saturday Night Live* played the clown role, where he literally dressed as a clown for the laughter and applause of the small yet influential New York City audience. Nowadays, Rock can command the attention of thousands of people with his presence alone, without gimmicks; his talent is now proof of his comic superiority and genius. However, if it were not for the clown role he played over twenty years ago, he may not be the international sensation he is today.

To be clear, I see no problem with someone performing a menial role in order to set themselves up for the future. However, I do have a problem with influential persons relying on an oversimplified formula of degeneracy with the expectation of never progressing for not only their audience's sake, but for their own.

Me Against the World

"Take that monkey shit off
You embarrassing us." [1]

• Pimp C •

n the past century, whites may have purely looked towards black people for entertainment and could not relate to the lifestyle of the Negro at that time. Now, we see whites still have challenges identifying with African Americans not only through entertainment, but human suffering. In *Sister Citizen: Shame, Stereotypes*, and *Black Women in America*, Melissa Harris-Perry identifies how months after Hurricane Katrina, blacks and whites saw the same horrific tragedy in two different perspectives. Blacks, when surveyed by a Pew research study, responded that racial inequality was still prevalent in America, government response to Katrina was fair or poor, and if victims had been white, the response would have been quicker. Whites, when asked these questions, responded similarly to the black participants in the survey, but at a much lower percentage. This confirmed while the two races literally saw the same coverage and effects of the storm, their point of views remained different. [2]

"In short, while most white Americans saw the hurricane's aftermath as tragic, they understood it primarily as a natural disaster followed by technical and bureaucratic failures. Most black Americans saw it as a racial disaster. For black Americans, the catastrophe was not just a matter of slow government response; the lack of coordinated response was itself an indication that black people did not matter to the government." [3]

• Melissa Harris-Perry, Sister Citizen •

In 1936, a contemporary Christian-centered fantasy film named *The Green Pastures* was released. Its significance is that it was the first major all-black production in over five years at the time, so audiences were yearning for a contemporary and quality black film. *The Green Pastures* would deliver, and according to film expert Donald Bogle, ". . . independently produced all-Negro features had revealed that there was a growing Negro audience eager for any product remotely touching on their own experiences." [4]

In this film, Negro actors played biblical characters and steered far away from any controversial subject matter, which pleased Negro audiences. They supported it seemingly regardless of the fact the actors were still depicted as misspoken and second rate citizens; Noah even wore a top hat and raincoat. Playing on the religious sensibilities of the black community and infusing the modern aesthetics of blackness, this film gave the black audience two things they could embrace without question: a religion they had always been told was right and people who looked like them. Since our arrival to America, we have been taught Christian principles and how to practice these things in order to reach our spiritual peak or heaven when we die. Spirituality, among other things, was taught in order for us to emulate the virtues of whites, supposedly making us better people in the process. Fast forwarding years and years, few things have remained in African American culture that existed in the days of slavery, reconstruction, the Civil Rights Era, and our present day more than Christianity.

I can remember in my fall 2004 semester at Winston Salem State University, there was hysteria over a tour of black theatre coming to our area with a host of black actors, producers, and a director who was an actor himself. It was reminiscent of the "chitlin circuit," a network of smaller and localized venues across the nation in which amateur black entertainers could display their talents and perform in front of their target audiences. This new cultural phenomenon was called "Madea." We did not know much about the on-stage plays except that they were good. The plays had made a name for themselves through word of mouth and slowly but surely evolved into the multi-million dollar enterprise it is today. For me, it was not until Tyler Perry reached the big screen that I was able to fully engage in a conversation about his themes, caricatures, and propagation. I can remember his first movie I saw was the 2007 release, *Why Did I Get Married*; I came away entertained, yet puzzled. I wondered: How could someone have such an introspective look on black women's feelings, thoughts, and insecurities? Then I remembered his claim to fame was made by portraying a woman.

I do not agree with the majority of Tyler Perry's projects and I will give reasons for my perspective. However, before I begin I must address the issue of "black on black" criticism and the "crabs in a barrel" mentality so many have stated we as blacks bestow upon each other. One of the major contemplations I had prior to writing this chapter was whether my criticism would be misconstrued by the reader as simply another "black on black" critique. It is popularly believed we, as blacks, are continually in competition with each other, therefore we are envious of each other's successes and instead of focusing on our own future and how to work together, we solely look to excoriate someone we feel is not worthy of the praise and acclaim they have received. I am not quite sure why this assertion is still relevant, as if a white journalist or writer would feel awkward for critiquing the works of a white director or scenarist, so why should we feel any different?

I think there is an overdue obligation for Perry's target audience to speak out about his work, which caters directly to them through cultural experiences, mannerisms, sassiness, religion, family structure, and relationships. If I am to dissect his work, I am obligated to do so intelligently and not as an impulsive and ill-informed viewer merely against all things Tyler Perry. But I have made it a point to learn as much as possible about those who came before him and how this current social climate measures to that of the past. That is why it was important for me to include the previous chapters, in order to illustrate the challenges we have overcome to rise to our current position in Hollywood, while also magnifying those who have had to dumb themselves down in order to be laughed at by nationwide audiences. There has been a concerted effort from many organizations and persons to dispel the many depictions of African Americans on television and movie screens.

Since *Birth of A Nation*, black people have been struggling with their representation on film and have been correcting the damage done over the years by Hollywood which has purposefully categorized black men as inferior. For example, during a 2006 interview with Oprah, comedian Dave Chappelle told a story about arguing with white men over wearing a dress in a particular movie scene, and his strong stance against it. Chappelle stated he could not understand why they were so adamant about him wearing a dress. He mentioned that the producer, director, and writer all tried to convince him the scene would be better if he wore the dress; however, he stood firm and did not budge. Minutes later, according to Chappelle, someone came back with a new script. Chappelle inferred they must have had a backup script waiting in the event he turned down the original idea.

It is not my intention to besmirch Perry's name or legacy. It is my purpose to offer a different perspective of his films; a perspective in which I feel I am not alone. Let us remember, even though I am critical of his work, if there was no Tyler Perry, there would be no world-renowned African American filmmaker to critique aside from Spike Lee, so with that being said, here is my two cents.

One of the biggest mistakes we can make as moviegoers or appreciators of any entertainment is to believe the purveyors of our interest and amusement should be limited, pigeon holed, and not allowed to grow in their craft. This mistake is evident in mid-century minstrelsy performers such as Paul Robeson, Louis Armstrong, and Hattie McDaniel, who in addition to serving as a "mammy" for the majority of her Hollywood career, could also beautifully recite Shakespeare. This systematic racism has been at work since the founding of our country and continues to permeate our nation through the media and entertainment on a daily basis. It is not a coincidence that even today most television shows on the air are dominated by a white cast, producers, and directors with a token African American character thrown in that is still typically used for comic relief.

McDaniel, above all other stereotypical actors and actresses in Hollywood, has served as a backdrop for the modern minstrel shows we now see. Even though McDaniel, like her other black colleagues, had to conform to white assumptions and exaggerated stereotypes, she was also known to have a sassy attitude and a clever wit she could use to her advantage when performing. It was something highly unheard of in the days of white authority and black subservience; this was also apparent in Stepin Fetchit when he was able to convince Hollywood directors he could not read so he could ad-lib his own lines and improvise his performances. [5] When we see someone black in those days fulfilling a role which is demeaning and racially derogatory, we merely see the show for what it is, and that is the end of it. We know now, through the actors' recollections of those days, that they had to perform for white studio executives, white directors, and white producers to make a show to be broadcasted for white America. There was no budging in the argument to let blacks present themselves in a formal, authoritative, or even equal role, and if they were going to change the status quo, they had to succumb to the pressures of racism that the South created and to which Hollywood sold. These performers, according to Stepin Fetchit, dealt with racism and denigration in order to one day change the way the system worked and open up more doors for deserving black people to get their shot at stardom.

These mid-century films were only a couple of hours long, but the reflection of American culture and the themes presented lasted long after the credits rolled. Perhaps that is why Fetchit's black audience held a contemptuous view of what other writers and movie critics heralded and thought was exceptional work. They knew Fetchit was profiting from divisive stereotypes that were untrue and far more damaging to their reputation than to Fetchit's.

Hattie McDaniel, along with other black maids at that time, were known for their similar physical appearance—more specifically, a heavy set, dark skinned woman wearing an apron or nightgown. It is this blueprint which has continued to permeate American culture, whether through Aunt Jemima or, more popularly, Madea. Madea is emblematic of Southern religious convictions infused with the sass and pure ignorance for which successful minstrel actresses were once praised. McDaniel once represented a non-threatening and amusing caricature who knew her place and dared not step out of bounds for fear of being reprimanded by her superiors, thus reinforcing how blacks need not strive for a sense of independence and self-worth.

McDaniel often toed the line between sassy and "out of line" in her roles, but she was never afforded the luxury of completely speaking freely to her white actors and actresses on screen. McDaniel, the consummate professional, like most entertainers then and now, found it difficult to have time for both family and work. McDaniel once again showed that art was imitating life, because even though she portrayed a maid which surely made her famous, she also had practice doing so during her earlier years in Colorado where she actually cleaned the homes of white families.

The life of a maid or real life "mammy" was something so demanding and time consuming it caused one to miss a significant amount of family time and prevented one from building relationships as we know them today. Dick Gregory put it simply:

". . . But I wonder about my Momma sometimes, and all the other Negro mothers who got up at 6 A.M. to go to the white man's house with sacks over their shoes because it was so wet and cold. I wonder how they made it. They worked very hard for the man, they made his breakfast and they scrubbed his floors and they diapered his babies. They didn't have too much time for us." [6]

Even before the world would be introduced to McDaniel or Fetchit, they would know the first African American boxing heavyweight champion Jack Johnson. As a testament to the overt racism ever present in those days, during the sold-out boxing match which would declare him victorious over the "Great White Hope" Jim Jeffries, the film used to record the fight was stopped at the moment Jeffries was knocked out to preserve the belief that a black man could not defeat a white man at anything, especially on a platform as large as that. The day after Jack Johnson successfully defended his title against arch nemesis Jim Jeffries on July 4, 1910 in Reno, Nevada, the *Los Angeles Times* wrote to its readers:

A word to the black man
Do not point your nose too high
Do not swell your chest too much
Do not boast too loudly
Do not be puffed up
Let not your ambition be inordinate
Or take a wrong direction
Remember you have done nothing at all
You are just the same member of society you were last week
You are on no higher plane
Deserve no new consideration
And will get none
No man will think a bit higher of you
Because your complexion is the same
As that of the victor at Reno

This message speaks to the illogical and constant inferiority once spewed at African Americans, even in the face of their success. However, this outrage over a brief moment of black superiority would move well past the newspapers and into the streets where angry whites across the country killed celebratory blacks to compensate for their boy's loss and an overall sad day for white America. This was all occurring in the early 20th century. In a country where the Heavyweight Champion of the world was being discriminated against, one can only imagine the suffocating animosity and overt prejudice which actors and actresses faced, as this treatment was not only considered normal but was encouraged.

"Among the Negro middle class, scorn was even greater if the entertainers happened to be minstrel performers. Just as many churchgoing blacks vigorously denounced the blues as the devil's music, the Negro elite typically condemned minstrelsy's ethnic comedy as reprehensible and distorted—a detriment to racial progress." [7]

"Many agreed that caricatures of the black underclass had some basis in reality but felt that excess focus on the lowest stratum of Negro life obscured the progress made by black professionals; they argued that suppressing those crude, comically exaggerated images was essential to uplifting the race and gaining respectability in the larger society." [8]

• Mel Watkins •

This quotation most precisely describes my individual disposition regarding Tyler Perry's movie, television, and stage career exploits. While I applaud his successes and the many careers he has helped to launch, when one breaks down his actual work, there are similarities of his message which not only mimic the days of minstrelsy but also seem to recreate new racist imagery. It is my belief, as I have seen firsthand, blacks and whites are not only entertained by his works but some believe them to be accurate portrayals of themselves, and in some cases, even pretend to be the characters they see.

Even though Stepin Fetchit, originally born as Lincoln Theodore Monroe Andrew Perry, was obviously intelligently gifted, the culture of the U.S. would not allow anti-stereotypical depictions of African Americans. What Fetchit was doing at that time was as common as a Will Ferrell comedic performance today. While Fetchit did help to create the images of blacks in the 20th century, the system was bigger than himself, and as a result, he had to conform to the images and culture of that time, just as Columbia Law Graduate Paul Robeson did.

By many accounts, Stepin Fetchit and Tyler Perry share an affinity for their religious belongings. While Tyler Perry chose to exhaust the different hymns and melodies in his music and solve his characters' problems through a predictable bible verse and melody, Fetchit never used religion to exploit his culture, even though that may have been the most appropriate time in theatrical history to do so. Fetchit was said to have a deep love for church during his childhood, yet it never materialized into a signature or even a recognizable part of his act.

In several of his columns in the *Chicago Defender*, he commented on pleasing God, getting one's life together, and spoke at length of the after-life once a fellow entertainer passed. [9] Another similarity between the two is their rite of entertainment passage to the unprecedented stardom through vagabonding during their early adulthood and going around the "chitlin circuit" so many aspiring black entertainers continue to travel today. Both Perry's started their careers off in small crowds, traveling to audiences in various locations who would watch them perform for little to no money in order to gain the experience and reputation of a must-see act.

White actors exemplified this as well, such as 20th century movie star Humphrey Bogart, who was cast to do a gangster film shortly after the Prohibition era took its course. Al Capone left a mark on not only the Chicago streets, but on the big screen—in this instance, art proves to be an imitation of life. Movies such as *The Public Enemy* (1931), *City Streets* (1931), *Scarface* (1932), *Angels with Dirty Faces* (1938) were all films which stayed current as they reflected the uprising of mob culture in the Prohibition era. The only difference is while those movies are seen as brief moments in history, both Tyler and Lincoln Perry's films are ingested as an indisputable staple of African American people, past and present.

As we moved into the 1940s, there was a changing perspective of African Americans in our country. These demeaning depictions were becoming challenged by more and more persons of influence—this became increasingly apparent once we entered World War II. It was not until World War II that black people were given the rights and privileges of an ordinary soldier. Even though they were not given much respect for their capabilities, it is undeniable that blacks, such as the now famous Tuskegee Airmen, helped to shift expectations of themselves, not only militarily but also for civilians. Blacks were granted an opportunity to prove they too were capable of training, carrying out missions, fighting for their country, and leading soldiers to victory. With this unprecedented look at what African Americans were capable of doing, it made the incessant motion pictures of Stepin Fetchit all the more ludicrous and misleading. This was a time when blacks were celebrated amongst each other for becoming doctors, inventors, lawyers, soldiers, and businessmen across the country, and all of these developments worked together in order to disprove the myths of black inferiority, slothfulness, complacency, and servitude.

"Black leaders and returning servicemen would demand America's overt recognition of their rights and equal status under the law. Its possible rewards notwithstanding, the venerable trickster ploy was rapidly losing credence in the black community." [10]

• Mel Watkins •

There had been attempts to shut down these Hollywood studios and their blatant disregard for positive black themes, but this particular time proved different. With Hitler's vociferous tirade and massacre of anyone other than German descendants, America was slowly loosening its stance on the racism and oppression which had defined the country for centuries. Additionally, "All-American" movie star Humphrey Bogart and the NAACP protested Hollywood's bias against black actors so they could finally be seen as proficient, competent, and equal. Our country was finally thinking progressively. We began to see changes in the real world and demanded they be illustrated in the entertainment industry as well. Hollywood producers were faced with an ultimatum to either change the theme of their movies and television shows or cancel their programs altogether—they chose the latter. Once the television show *Amos 'n' Andy* was taken off the air in the mid 1960s, it marked the end of an era that was already outdated.

As Perry is the only African American director who is currently directing and acting in blockbuster movies on an annual basis, his truth and perspective have become America's truth and perspective. Whether these images and themes are consistent with the actual population being exploited is irrelevant, because what is being signified is that these images are in fact true. The power of a black director in Hollywood is something which cannot be understated; he single-handedly dictates the perceptions of his culture and whatever he feels necessary to perpetuate will be enforced on-screen and off-screen over a period of time by the viewing public. After these recurring motifs have been presented with very little deviation, they become normal and expected from persons inside and outside of that culture.

I have heard the argument that Tyler Perry is giving people jobs who may have not been able to work otherwise, and I can appreciate his willingness to promote his own people on and off screen. However, at what cost is this employment gained? Is the cost not bigger than the gain? Is that really the only excuse for allowing one man's subjective view of his people to be continually categorized? To paraphrase what social commentator Toure' stated in a CNN interview in 2011, drug dealers can create jobs but that does not make them "good jobs." Toure' also called Perry's work "cinematic malt liquor;" a view I cannot fully support as I do think there is a usefulness in his roles, though I do see how one can draw such a conclusion upon considering the roles Perry chooses to highlight. [11] In contrast, one of Tyler Perry's most visible and known supporters, Rev. Al Sharpton, vehemently defends his work and even honored Perry in the 2011 National Action Network at the Triumph Awards, calling Perry's critics "proper Negroes" who don't understand black folk. *The Washington Post* reported that Sharpton presented the typical argument for Perry by stating that he has given jobs to blacks who would not have otherwise worked in Hollywood and created his own empire. The newspaper also quoted Perry:

> *". . . Instead of getting your education and running from us, you need to ground and root yourself in who we are. Every other culture in this country knows the value of us as black people but we don't know it ourselves."* [12]

Firstly, Perry misses the mark completely. What he is saying is: if we do not agree with the themes and motifs of his films, you are somehow unaware of the apparent and natural state of black people in America; as if his films contain the essence of all things black and those who challenge that holistic culture are no longer grounded by blackness but rather by formal education. It implies one cannot be formally educated and still appreciate his movies, which is indicative of who and what he represents as a filmmaker. If a people with higher degrees of education, much like the characters in most of his plays, does not like the content and portrayals of his movies, is he rightful to believe they are all uppity and snobbish towards anything that does not reflect blacks as high-class or aristocratic? No one likes to see their people degraded to the lowest forms of what they have already been portrayed as. For those who did not experience a higher level of education, they may not know the history of earlier century minstrel show performers who walk, talk, and act like Perry's characters, Madea and Mr. Brown. Using education, a resource many of us did not have access to in past decades, as an excuse for his subpar films is something which ought to be beneath a man who makes it a point to advertise the social and professional benefits of education in many of his film's characters.

Also, his quote implies if one is educated, one is automatically uplifted into a higher stratosphere overlooking all things black. As if once someone of color earns a degree from an institution of higher learning, they completely disavow everything that made them black.

This "us" versus "them" mentality only serves to falsely perpetuate the idea that the black bourgeoisie will distance themselves from lower to middle class African Americans. I find this appalling because many persons, like myself, who are not the most financially empowered are still critical of Perry's work, and yes, it is because of education. Historically Black Colleges and Universities in particular, provide black students with the confidence and appreciation of their own history they otherwise may not acquire elsewhere, and we learn from that history. One need not be a president, CEO, or board member to see Perry's most popular works contain demeaning and condescending messages which have to be addressed and not blindly supported for the sole purpose of supporting him because he is black. If a black person chooses to educate themselves, why should they be castigated and categorized as "proper Negroes" or "running from" our own kind?

Furthermore, his second point in which he mentions we are unaware of our own culture's worth, but other cultures are, is a complete farce and delusion from reality. If we are going to be frank, with a history as rich and purposefully hidden as our own, no one can truthfully say outsiders know the value of us better than we ourselves. To truly know and understand the depths of African American history and modernity, one has to thoroughly seek that knowledge out, as it is not provided in grade school or broadcast on television. With that knowledge, one may gain a sense of appreciation for our people's tragedies and triumphs; however, the average person is unaware of these historical realities. This is not to suggest all blacks are culturally introspective, as we have our fair share of people who could care less about their own history and how it impacts their present existence. There is a wide spread absence of knowledge of the persons that influenced blacks in our country and the month of February is hardly enough to cover it.

In an October 2009 interview with 60 Minutes when speaking of Madea and Mr. Brown, Perry said, ". . . these characters are bait, disarming, charming, make-you-laugh bait so I can slap Madea in something and talk about God, love, faith, forgiveness, family—any of those things." Perry, over the course of his career, has not shied away from Christian values and infusing his characters and storylines with controversies that are often solved by relying on those very values.

Perry has made the Bible as synonymous to his name as a night-gown. Nonetheless, by constantly choosing to display praise and proselytizing behaviors from himself and many of his actors, Perry is making a conscious effort to exclude certain persons from his viewing public. After seeing one or two Madea films, the audience is aware of the themes which will be featured in the movies, and Perry has stated it is his purpose to make God the focal point in his films. The result is, over time the audience realizes what they are witnessing is not new but rather re-packaged material with new characters, new loca-tions, and new catch phrases, yet with the same old Madea and the same dull script they have heard before. Perry, to this point, has used

Christianity to validate the antics and lack of creativity featured in his films, and if not for the loyal consumer base he has built over the last decade, he may actually have to challenge his creative parameters and introduce something of value, substance, and relevance. Perry has used nearly every bible verse, correctly and incorrectly, in his films to justify his work, and the core audience continues to absorb the films; however, more should be required of him.

Perry may have noble intentions by interjecting many Christian values in his movies, television shows and stage plays; however, that is not the takeaway from his productions. What Perry fails to recognize is that the everlasting message of his most popular works is the actual "bait," and it tends to overshadow the more serious and often dramatic performances of his projects. It is apparent in his advertisements for the Madea plays and movies that they appeal to a certain type of audience; if one were to look at a poster of one of his stage plays, one would expect nothing less than a knee-slapping good time, not a critical examination of love and faith between two people.

It is clear Tyler Perry is talented, but he is doing himself and his audience a disservice by serving us the same garbage our country once thought was an accurate depiction of blacks. It makes one wonder if blacks will one day, like they did once Fetchit's career was over, denounce his works. There came a time when Fetchit himself was no longer accepted, as his roles began to illustrate the same monotonous images of a lazy, easily fooled "coon" that was at one time his bread and butter. [13]

Chapter 7: Me Against the World

". . . Black Americans had turned a deaf ear to his previous accomplishments and generally regarded him with no more respect than that bestowed on Aunt Jemima or those venerable uncles, Tom and Ben." [14]

• Mel Watkins •

One consistency among Stepin Fetchit was his intolerability throughout his career on Hollywood sets. Even with discrimination, prejudice, and overt racism, he still managed to assert demands for himself as a top paid actor. There were few actors who could compete with his tomfoolery, dancing, and utter stupidity, so many times he was given another "second chance" strictly because of his talents. At several points, Fetchit expressed his frustrations with Hollywood studios' tendency to propagate stereotypes more than the previous film and continually give him hyperbolically inferior roles. Though Fetchit was a catalyst in black stereotypes on the big screen, even he insisted he grew tired of portraying his culture as merely mentally inferior and lazy servants. Fetchit would even go as far as suing CBS, Xerox, Twentieth Century Fox, and the Indiana Broadcasting Company in which he explained a 1968 character he portrayed as "the white man's Negro." [15] This is something that was not clearly stated in the previous years; one had to conform to what the studios wanted, a point well made by author Mel Watkins when speaking about Fetchit's roles:

"But the lessons learned from Fetchit's unpredictable behavior and aggressive, demanding stance with the industry bigwigs—resulting in what was essentially an across-the-board blackballing at major studios—most surely have influenced them as well. The message was clear. Toe the line or leave." [16]

Let us also remember Fetchit's film career took off in the early 1930s, a time when America was trying to recover from the stock market crash and consequential Great Depression. Much like the Recession of 2008, black people were among the most critically affected population, giving proof of the popular adage, "Last hired, First fired." Blacks, in some cases, had no other choice but to take these roles, not only to further their career, but to put food in their mouths.

This was a common complaint amongst Fetchit's critics, who vehemently denounced his works as nothing more than servitude on a silver screen. On the other hand, much like Tyler Perry, while compromising his integrity and talents, Fetchit also opened doors for other actors who would follow after him. His contemporaries such as "Stomp n Sellit," "Pigmeat Markham," "Buck and Bubbles," and others profited from his works and innovation just as Tyler Perry now has successors of his plays who use Christian-themed dramas and comedies to emulate Perry's successful line of stage and silver screen performances. Though Fetchit received an enormous amount of backlash during and after his film career, he did open many doors for other actors to broadcast their talents and add a level of diversity to the roles not granted to him upon his entrance into Hollywood. It is true Fetchit was the highest paid black actor of his time, but the price he ended up paying for his caricatures far outlasted his monetary gains.

Another major motivation for writing this book was the movie trailer I saw for Tyler Perry's 2011 release, *Madea's Big Happy Family*. During this particular preview, they showed Maury Povich, a syndicated television show host, would be featured in the upcoming film.

Maury Povich, in my opinion, is worse than Sheriff Joe Arpaio and Larry Elder mixed in with a sprinkle of Stron Thurman; so for Tyler Perry to reach out to him and request his help in further dumbing down his people is something that must be addressed. *The Maury Show*, as far as I can tell, is the biggest and longest running minstrel show in our modern television era. To sum up his show, on a typical day 1) a woman comes out (usually black), 2) says she has had sexual relationships with several men, 3) those men come out (usually black), 4) they all argue about how each other is wrong, and finally 5) they reveal who the real "father" is through paternity testing, and when it is revealed the said men are NOT the father—they express an unrestrained jubilance that is only comparable to a child on Christmas morning. If a man is found to be the "father," then he typically sucks it up and says a generic message such as "Imma take care of my responsibility as a man." The real kicker comes when no man is the father and the mother has no clue who her child's father is. At that particular time, the men on the show can point, shuck and jive, knowing they have dodged the infamous bullet of actually having to take care of a child they helped create. When this image is continually displayed, it becomes normal and expected, so when persons do not engage in those practices, they are seen as abnormal.

In Fetchit's life, he also publicly underwent a marital scandal and controversially announced the son he had taken care of for so long was actually not his. There was an ongoing court battle in which Fethcit accused his former wife of being promiscuous and challenged her character, foreshadowing what minstrel day-time television would become decades later.

With that being said, it is easy to see how the combination of *The Maury Show* and Tyler Perry could create a historical disaster of epic proportions. With two entities that profit from the exploitation of blacks, it is a match made in entertainment Heaven. In those several minutes on *The Maury Show*, Madea tries to prove a man is the father of her child and, once the paternity test is shown, it is discovered he is not the father. Madea, like most guests, cries hysterically and runs backstage, collapsing in the process.

If you are reading this, you may think I am making more of this than it is worth; contrarily, it is due to these repeated stereotypes that we expect and demand these generalized and embellished actions of a typical *Maury Show*. If one of us rejects the premise of this falsified black culture, we are then seen as different, out of touch, or the dreaded "acting white."

Let us think about the impact of an entire population being defined by one person. What would his motivations be? By what measurement would he come to these characters? Who and what are they based upon? You see, Tyler Perry is doing what he knows, just as the Hughes Brothers, John Singleton, Gordon Parks, The Wayans Brothers, etc. have done. He is telling a story the best way he knows how based on his worldview.

The frequency and success in which Tyler Perry has released his films is unprecedented amongst black directors. He released twelve major motion pictures from 2005-2011, something no other African American director has been able to do. We, the people, have been inundated with his perspective of black culture, and as a consequence, our tolerance for his messages, on film or in real life, has become more acceptable and less questionable. When someone is not presented with an alternative message, he/she tends to cling to whatever is most popular because that is the only message being presented without any objection, critical thinking, or second guessing.

On an aesthetical level, you can also see the correlation between his characters and decades past. Before movies were aesthetically appealing as they have been for decades now, audiences did not have the benefit of hearing the characters they watched on film, and to compensate for the lack of audibility, actors had to exaggerate their body language and facial expressions in order to tell a story. Fetchit's later pictures would have audio, but for some time, his caricature and on-screen abilities carried the film far enough that sound was not needed. Today's example of "Mr. Brown" would have fit well in the days of minstrel shows. He would have been a top-shelf porch monkey through his schucking and jiving, wide smile, overly eccentric attire, easily fooled and manipulated innocence, dark skin, and proving to be an utter buffoon in every translation of the word. Mr. Brown epitomizes what the perception of blacks was in the days of *Amos 'n' Andy*, except now this is a black man portraying himself in this depleting manner by the direction of another black man.

Based on the aesthetic of Madea, we see she possesses the classic "mammy" characteristic which was popularly portrayed by Hattie McDaniel. The permanent nightgown, apparently fashionable everywhere, and the brazen ghetto-ness and outspoken demeanor allows her character the luxury of saying whatever she wants without consequence. The manner in which she behaves is something that was most popular in the old days; the habitual mispronunciation of words and the fact that she ties religion into any given storyline often comes off as forced and unnatural. Even if someone cannot relate to the storyline or characters, Tyler Perry assumes his audience is overly religious and wants to spontaneously go into worship during his plays and movies.

Are the Madea and Mr. Brown caricatures even partially accurate depictions of today? With so many advancements in the world from African Americans, how can his most well-known character possess none of those characteristics, educational achievements, or ambitions? What world is Tyler Perry living in where he sees a belligerent 6'5" gray-haired hot-tempered black woman walking around in a floral print nightgown, gun in her purse, and at the end of every foul-mouthed argument, uses a bible verse and southern gospel song to justify her "principles?"

Perry is more than capable of producing works that can represent black people with pride, dignity, and moral character. His television show on OWN, *The Haves and The Have Nots*, illustrates that he has the capacity to think outside of the box; however, when one thinks of Tyler Perry, this show is typically not recalled.

The success of his films beckons the question: Do we, the public, crave his movies? As black people, we have traditionally been the last ones to receive equality, and Hollywood is no different. In my mind, I thought because of the "spike" in black consciousness films in the last 20 years, we were past this stage of black on black ignorance. However, it seems we have regressed to a point far exceeding what was typical in the 1970s and 80s. Now it seems we have to dig ourselves out of a hole that has been dug by our own shovel.

The Wayans Brothers make fun of Hollywood by producing over-exaggerated depictions of black culture; they shine light on the illogicality of the system at work. Conversely, Tyler Perry uses those caricatures as a foundation to build his dynasty. It has become apparent he does not see his films as comedies but as serious dramas.

Jay-Z popularly released the track "Death of Auto-Tune" for his 2009 album *Blueprint III*, a song in which he informed all rappers that their trendy and synthesized singing was becoming saturated and effectively killed their style of rapping. Sometimes it takes a person of authority to make a point everyone knows needs to be stated in order for change to be made. As I mentioned before, the Wayans Bros. used past movies and the current influx of hood films to mock the culture of the times with *Don't Be a Menace to South Central While Drinking Your Juice in the Hood*, as that era came to an end. While they were parodying the very movies which were, in some degree, accurate portrayals of African American lifestyle, they also helped to demonstrate the illogicality, immaturity, and derisive nature of ghetto life through exaggerated comic relief and brazen racial overtones.

What is more disturbing about Perry's film career thus far is that there has been no visible progression in the messages he has presented. His film's quality has not evolved to showcase anything which would differentiate his first movie from the last. I understand the importance of pandering to your audience with what is familiar to them, nonetheless, he has failed to challenge his audience to think abstractly, and it is apparent in his work. After working for six years as a director, Spike Lee released *Do The Right Thing*. In comparison, in Perry's sixth year as the highest grossing black director in history, he released *Madea's Big Happy Family*. The two movies could not be more different but I am not looking to judge them on theme or importance, but the quality of story, characters, and production.

Another glaring theme is the apparent disapproval of black men which rears its head in a majority of his films, illustrating them as cheaters, jocks, chauvinistic, misogynistic, or unable to take care of a woman or family, let alone himself. Perry, for whatever reason, has zoned in on his audience without regard for the men he portrays as inadequate lovers and spouses.

Thus far Perry has demonstrated throughout his career that he has no intentions of being a figure which inspires introspection other than religious overreliance and relationship provocation. This may be according to his personal experiences and those nearest him, yet and still, his entire potential audience cannot relate to a jigging buffoon like Mr. Brown or a ghetto-fabulous figure like Madea.

While it may not be fair to compare each director by their own motivations for filmmaking, Perry may be under the impression that his films are just as important to the black community as Lee's *School Daze*. Consider the timeline of Tyler Perry's films. His first release was in 2005, and he has continued to create television shows, stage plays, and feature films ever since. During this time, African Americans have seen some of the lowest points in recent history, particularly regarding our economic standing, urban violence, healthcare inefficiencies, along with other problems significant to black people. Perry has made no effort, in the public eye, to address these issues. His power and earned privilege has not been used effectively to speak out and influence his people or guide his audience anywhere other than a movie theater. I am sure the *Tyler Perry Foundation* does great things for his community and persons in need of assistance, however, when we, the people, witness a lack of socio-political involvement and an overabundance of constant buffoonery and misrepresentation for years on end, what other conclusion can be drawn?

You do not have to be black to understand the emotional connection between the husband and wife in *Why Did I Get Married?* In the first movie, Marcus is disgusted by the weight his wife, Sheila, portrayed by Jill Scott, has gained over the years, but in the sequel, he expresses anger, jealousy, and regret after they have separated and she has moved on to someone else. That type of scenario can evoke emotions of empathy, karma, and vindication which could cause the moviegoer to think back to the one that got away, or even look inward at themselves to see whether they are too judgmental toward the people with whom they are connected. Also, in *Do The Right Thing*, one does not need to be black to understand Mookie and his relationship problems, time constraints, cultural differences at work, and negligence of his son. That is a telling sign concerning both of their creative geniuses. While they both present topics and stories usually geared towards an African American audience, the message of their productions can often be appreciated by people of all colors. No one is naive enough to think it is only black people who view their films or watch Perry's television series. It is completely understandable the themes and tones they present are accepted by different cultures, but the way it is interpreted is where the danger lies.

There are many instances in American History when we are fooled by what qualifies something or someone as racist; such as in 2013, when George Zimmerman was found "not guilty" of killing Trayvon Martin. The verdict was reached by a nearly all white female jury, and while no one knows their specific motivations and reasons for determining the verdict they selected, none of the jurors, I am sure, would identify themselves as racist, even though the case was clearly about race, as stated by one of the jurors. [17] The way messages are interpreted in today's movie culture speaks a lot to how our country chooses to accept racism. We see how movies, such as *The Butler* (2013), are successful because it illustrates that we as Americans have overcome the blatant and publicly demonstrated racism which was once based upon law. Most people, of all colors, can recognize and appreciate the progression. Additionally, these movies send a message that essentially says: because dogs are no longer chasing us, police are no longer beating us senseless in broad daylight, or arresting us for simply sitting down at a diner, racism is non-existent. On the contrary, we see how the murder, plea, and verdict of civil cases such as that of Trayvon Martin, demonstrate racism and prejudice are very much alive and well. There are countless acts of racism against black people which are far too vast to name, but the root cause of such discriminations are the false perceptions and the lowered expectations we often have of each other as well, resulting in a constant fight for the most basic rights, freedoms, opportunities, and privileges that go along with being an American citizen.

A director who constructs his own legacy from one message, and nothing else, is a phenomenon usually received with praise and amazement or disinterest and ridicule. Art is an evolving form, and when a director, painter, orchestrator, or musician chooses to settle with the bare minimum or basic fundamentals of his or her achievement, it lulls the growth of not only the creator of the works, but also of his or her respective audience and most adamant supporters.

Perry has proven over the years he is smart enough to remain relevant in the minds of Americans and continuously provide a story which speaks to his audience with his modern interpretation of African American culture. What is less clear about Tyler Perry is the direction of his filmmaking in the future. In a 2011 interview with Mo'nique on BET, when asked how long he would keep making Madea movies, he responded with: "as long as people want to see her, she'll be around." While I can appreciate his efforts in being a black man with unprecedented success, I have to objectively look at the quality of material being presented, and thus far, there is a lack of substance none of his Madea-themed movies have been able to improve upon. I cannot say for certain if he is doing this merely for profit, but I do believe anyone who has a talent should be motivated by not only profits but by outdoing his or her own success.

What we have seen through Perry's consistent Madea films is a repeated and overtly simplistic platform to display the African American struggle and ultimate triumph through the implementation of Christianity mixed in with the ever-important Madea or Mr. Brown characters that validate Christianity ideologies using "shuck and jive" anachronisms. It is a successful formula, but with that formula derives an expectation from one's audience; they expect something they can rely upon and relate to, as much as the person playing that character. This is demonstrated by Perry's films which attempt to have respectability in a world outside of his loyal audience.

In October 2012, Perry was the lead actor in the best-selling novel action thriller turned motion picture *Alex Cross*, directed by Rob Cohen, where he played a Psychologist/Detective who investigates the murder of his wife slain by a serial killer. Though Perry did not direct or produce the film, he did star in it and appear in the television commercials, print ads, and interviews for the film. His promotional visibility for *Alex Cross* was similar to that of any Madea film; however, this film would not yield the same results. *Alex Cross* would be Perry's second lowest grossing film of his career, first belonging to his 2007 drama *Daddy's Little Girls*. *Alex Cross* earned just over $11 million during its weekend release, in comparison to his Madea films which average over $30 million in their opening weekends. His 2014 film, *The Single Mom's Club*, which was written and directed by Perry, would produce less than each of those on it is opening weekend, earning a disappointing $8.3 million. This film would mark the end of Perry's partnership with LionsGate as it is reported Perry will begin focusing more on television endeavors with the OWN Network.

The fact is: even when he tries to maintain a certain level of credibility and seriousness throughout a film, without interjections of comic relief, his own audience will not support it as he has made it a staple of who he is. I do not believe this to be exclusive to Tyler Perry; many actors are typecast into action roles such as Jason Statham or boisterous/violent roles like Samuel L. Jackson. Notwithstanding, persons such as Perry who have literally built an empire on stage plays, motion pictures and television shows are forever categorized, and once he takes off the fat suit, lipstick, and gown, it becomes hard to recognize him as another character, as proven by his bleak sales of *Alex Cross*.

So many times we hear the simple analogy of African Americans being crabs in a barrel pulling each other down, therefore, no one advances and they are all stuck in the same place. This analogy was used yet again when Spike Lee chose to talk about Tyler Perry's movies, television shows, and motives in an interview in December of 2009 when he stated Perry's work is "coonery and buffoonery." [18] He also states Perry is smart and gave him credit for his insight and perseverance to become the success he is. Lee insists it is the imagery of what Perry presents with which he has the problem. With the examples given from both of their movies, one can see this analogy does not serve either man properly as they both have different life experiences which have built the foundation for the types of movies they want to create. It is undeniable that both men are genius at their craft, but one must understand they are two entirely different people with two entirely different motivations and creativities.

It was important for Lee to come out and speak on Perry's works, more so than I or any other cultural critic. In this instance, you have someone who has done and seen it all twice over, someone who knows the movie industry inside out and can relate to the plight and creative struggle only a black Hollywood director could understand. So with that, Lee should be able to challenge him on the merits of his work and have a discussion about the consistent topics being presented. This criticism could be described as constructive if Perry chose to see it that way, but when he later responded that "Spike Lee can go straight to hell," it initially confirmed Perry did not take the criticism as constructive, but as a personal attack on his character. [19] Lee questioned the imagery of his work, not who Perry is as a man or human being. I believe this to be another example of how we as blacks, use race as a scapegoat to explain things we do not agree with and cannot disprove with our actions or logic; rather some of us choose to be dismissive using oversimplified and traditional excuses.

When it comes to producing a quality picture, the two could not be more different. While Perry makes movies and television shows that only blacks can relate to firsthand, Lee opens his mind and provides perspectives from black culture which can be appreciated by all people. Such is the case for Lee's 1983 first feature film, *Joe's Bed-Stuy Barbershop: We Cut Heads* which was awarded the Locarno International Film Festival Award and for which Lee would subsequently go on to be nominated and win awards in Mexico, Germany, France, UK, and Spain. Lee has also been nominated for multiple Golden Globes, two Academy Awards, along with being nominated and winning several Cannes Film Festival awards amongst a plethora of other awards, domestic and abroad. Perry, on the other hand, has customarily won national accolades within the U.S. from a majority of black organizations (NAACP Image Awards, Black Reel Awards, BET Comedy Awards, Black Movie Awards, Acapulco Black Film Festival), proving it is only his core audience who finds his work to be award worthy. Perry also received a nomination from the MTV Movie Awards for Best

Comedic Performance in *Madea's Family Reunion* in 2006, verifying his value to that audience is that of nothing more than a figure to laugh at, not the Christian principles and life lessons he often presents in his films. This is not to suggest one needs worldwide or outside approval for validation, but it does speak volumes when an international audience can recognize great filmmaking and the picture does not consist of a popular or mainstream message.

Every generation has its own songs, dances, and images, and the people react to it accordingly. Tyler Perry is speaking to this generation of consumers about issues he believes to be as important as any other project on the market. While he typically uses the Madea caricature to sell tickets, his movies attempt to provide his target audience with a balanced view of themselves, their presumed religion, and characteristics. I, as only one of the members of his target audience, expected to see more of his creativity and not solely one message or one point of view. As I stated in chapter one, we as black people do not have many known persons of notoriety in the film industry behind the cameras, which makes it more difficult to reach every spectrum of the African American audience equally. However, when a director shows complacency through his or her art, it insults the intelligence of certain people in his audience. While some may like the consistent "coonery and buffoonery," there is also another segment of our population who has grown tired of this cinematic stagnation and wants to see where he can take his talents.

It is not as if Perry is unaware of the plight of his community and does not have a conscience, as evidenced by his dramatic productions of *Precious* (2009) and *For Colored Girls* (2010), where he tugs at the heartstrings of audiences, illustrating issues that often go unspoken of in the African American community, including depression, self-hate, incest, suicide, low self-esteem, and other emotions the average moviegoer can relate to. What is most of all needed from Perry is not necessarily more movies such as these, but rather films which can diversify his brand while also providing his audience with a chance to see just how great he can be.

Perry did not get where he is today by being lazy or slothful in his approach to filmmaking, but with success comes scrutiny and if he is to elevate his legacy beyond a director capable of only successfully relating to his audience through gimmick, stereotype, and misnomers, he will have to become more motivated by the realities of his culture and how those realities shapes their worldview.

As proven by his ticket sales, it is clear his audience is a direct reflection of the type of works Perry creates. Seven of his top ten highest grossing films include Madea and the characters we have all grown to know while the last one features predictable themes of black dysfunction and relationship problems with seemingly every member of the main cast.

The Madea Factory

1. Madea Goes to Jail

In this film, Madea is featured quite regularly throughout, as it is one of her most flagrant and boisterous performances to date. The film's central story is about a young black woman, Candice, who walks and works the streets until she meets up with her childhood friend, Josh, now a lawyer, who eventually saves her from the downward spiral which has become her life. Josh and Candice reminisce about growing up when times were simpler, then he eventually leaves his fiancé at the alter and chooses to be with Candice. In the midst of all the madness, Madea, along with the street walker, goes to jail and both are inevitably released. However, during the course of the movie, Madea hits a car for cutting her daughter off in traffic, then goes to Dr. Phil for her anger and benefits none from the visit as she resumes her usual ignorant and combative characteristics. She later retaliates toward a woman who stole a K-Mart parking spot from her. By operating a forklift, Madea lifts and drops the woman's car onto the pavement, an act of violence she is later arrested for. At her sentencing, she argumentatively back talks, kicks and screams until she is forcefully escorted out of the courtroom by bailiffs.

The movie, not bad by all accounts, is however dumbed down by the constant antics and utter stupidity which constantly interrupts the storyline. In each of Perry's Madea films, her antics are much more brazen and foolish than the picture before, which creates a cycle of tomfoolery that is in an ever-increasing perpetual state of idiocy. When we watch a movie like *Dumb & Dumber* (1994), it is understood what we are seeing is a comedy because there is no subtext, no underlying message of good will towards mankind, or sociopolitical message associated with it. However, in the *Madea Goes to Jail* and most other Madea films, she interjects, as Perry intends, to infuse the story with light-hearted fun and preposterous antics which instantly strips the picture of any sort of credibility.

2. Madea's Family Reunion

This Madea picture is not unlike most others where black males are either seen as possessive, troubled, and/or violent towards the women they claim to love. The protagonist, Carlos, is reminiscent of the character in Perry's first film, Charles in Diary of a Mad Black Woman, whom is seen as a successful and confident man by outsiders, however, behind closed doors he is insecure, petty, and can only express himself through physically harming a woman. Even when Charles' fiancé, Lisa, approaches her mother, a gold-digging ex-prostitute, about being hit by Carlos, her mother tells her to settle with him and accuses her of being "just like your no-good father, who walked out on me." Again, Perry continually perpetuates the misconception that a black man is not a responsible father and husband.

Predictably, Madea intervenes just as previous "coon" caricatures would do last century to infuse the storyline with comedy and relieve it of being considered a quality film. This time, Madea appears in court for removing her ankle bracelet and is ordered to take in a foster child. Initially, Madea and the female foster kid do not get along, however, over time they begin to accept and appreciate each other. The young girl tells Madea that she's being bullied on the way to school and later Madea enters the school bus and attacks one of the black teenage boys for talking back to her. Everybody on the bus laughs and cheers her on as Madea jumps on the boy, slapping and pushing him; again, reinforcing the value that a black male has in his films which are in constant need of reprimand and correction.

Lisa' sister, Vanessa, has had her guard up for a majority of the film, and is reluctant to trust another black man, Frankie, who wants to be there for her and her two children. Vanessa eventually gives in and allows herself to vulnerable enough to find love with him, though it would take much pursuing and convincing through Frankie's words and actions.

Lisa and Carlos are later at a dinner with friends, where they once again are about to have another fight, and Lisa dares him to hit her like he does in their home so people can see what he is really like. Later that night at home, Lisa threatens to leave Carlos and he opens the balcony window, stating that is the only way she's leaving and nearly throws her over. Lisa eventually escapes and retreats to Madea's home where Madea gives her the advice to "cook breakfast for him" and once he is comfortable, say "good morn-ting" and throw a pot of boiling grits on him. Tyler Perry has continually created in his Madea films the perception that men are mostly dangerous alpha males, deceivers and monstrous and rarely empathetic, sensitive, or well-intentioned and instead of repairing the situation, it is best to leave them without resolution.

Later in the film Lisa and Vanessa's mother, Victoria, admits that their father was a molester and pedophile, as Vanessa mentions that he raped her as a child and it has affected her relationships with men as an adult. The mother acknowledges that he raped her but justified it solely because he also provided for the family.

Perry later attempts to save the film by interjecting well-known and iconic black figures at the Family Reunion such as Maya Angelou and Cicely Tyson which offer wisdom and insight, along with a predictable Negro spiritual, but by this point in the film—all hope is lost.

Fast forward to the wedding day of Lisa and Carlos, they both meet at Madea's home and when Carlos strikes her once again, Lisa takes Madea's advice and throws a pot of grits on him and hits Carlos with an iron skillet, canceling the wedding in the process. Frankie and Vanessa end up getting married later that day as the movie ends and Perry gives the audience exactly what they want and nothing new.

3. Tyler Perry Presents Madea's Witness Protection

This film is not unlike Perry's other Madea pictures which feature her usual loud and boisterous antics and mannerisms. In this particular story, a wealthy white family enters a witness protection program and are housed at Madea's home and surprise surprise, she "blackens" them up before they leave and effectively teaches the mother to speak as "black" as she does. Later in the picture, the mother uses her newfound slang to tell her pushover husband to stand up for himself, screaming in a Madea voice, amongst other things, ". . . Hell, get yo ass together, you heard me, hell!" in the most profoundly horrible white-person-imitating-a-black-person voice that I have ever seen or heard. Earlier, in Madea's first appearance on camera, she is leaving the grocery store whilst complaining about using her EBT card so normally as if it is the only method of payment accepted in grocery stores. It is a fact that blacks use food stamps at a far less rate than whites, but because of these constant and inaccurate portrayals of us, it goes unchallenged and expected. It ends as is customary in Madea films, with a southern and soul-filled church song as a symbol that all is good as the family returns to their normal life, as does Madea.

4. Tyler Perry's Why Did I Get Married?

As a movie which focuses on the relationships of four different black couples, this film serves as a legitimate Drama which explores different dynamics everyday people encounter such as communication, humiliation, constant nagging, jealousies, and other unresolved issues. With black people in a variety of backgrounds, experiences, and professions, Perry presents a melting pot of our own culture and characters who are relatable to the audience. By doing this, Perry also humanizes them in a way which allows the viewer an opportunity to have a conversation with their significant other who may or may not exhibit the characteristics seen on screen.

5. Tyler Perry's Diary of a Mad Black Woman

In Perry's first feature film, *Diary Of A Mad Black Woman*, the story follows the life of Helen, the wife of the powerful and acclaimed Atlanta attorney simply known as Charles. Publicly, Charles is a highly successful family man who has a balance of life, family, and work; yet when alone, the two of them know the real "Charles" can be verbally and physically abusive. His wife is clearly portrayed as the victim; even when she asks him about infidelity, he tells her to pay a bill before questioning his decisions. Later, he confirms her suspicions on their anniversary by showing up to their home with his new girlfriend and two children he has fathered, and subsequently drags his wife out of the house with her belongings already packed outside. She later meets the moving truck driver, Orlando, who tries to sympathize with her but she is so enraged with her husband she kicks Orlando out of his own truck and drives herself to Madea's home.

As Helen arrives in the middle of the night, Madea opens the door firing shots from her handgun in a belligerent tirade which introduces her character to the silver screen. A few *Color Purple* references later, Madea chastises her for not having a prenuptial agreement; Helen later admits she has been getting beaten by Charles. At this point Madea brings Helen along to take her things back from her old home by breaking through the security gate and going into her old closet which is now the new girlfriend's closet. They proceed to tear the clothes down; Madea then takes a moment to pause and screams, "This is for every black woman who ever had a problem with a black man!" Inadvertently implying men who have ever hurt a black woman deserve to have their property destroyed which casts a wide net over the entire black male audience, all of whom he surely must not believe has done harm to black women.

They later interject with Madea's comic relief in the court scene. Orlando later enters the scene again but Helen is still so upset she throws her drink in his face when he tries to talk to her. More Madea comic relief ensues. Helen later apologizes to Orlando for throwing the drink in his face.

Later, Helen visits her mother in the nursing home where she is told she does not need a man to complete her and reaffirms to her that God is all that matters in her life. Helen and Orlando later speak at the restaurant Helen is now working at as an independent woman. Shortly thereafter, a soulful church scene interjects with "Jesus will work it out" as the chorus plays. After a while, she softens up to Orlando and is able to put her past relationship behind her.

Perry's latest Madea film, *Tyler Perry's A Madea Christmas* (2013) misses the mark as well, as many of his critics have pointed out. According to *TIME Magazine*'s Richard Corliss, "The only bright thing about the movie is the star's blindingly white teeth, which, if he smiles, could be seen from space. And the one fascination of *A Madea Christmas* is how little care the country's most popular and powerful indie filmmaker takes in shaping his own material. It's as if he looked at the low bar set by his earlier films and decided the challenge was to Limbo under it." Nicolas Rapold of *The New York Times* remarked, "With a character who can essentially say and do whatever she wants, you might expect a bit more." Tirdad Derakhshani of *The Philadelphia Inquirer* wrote, "Slapdash, with dialogue and plot points that were cliches in Dickens' era, the pic sends up, then reaffirms, all the values the media sell us each holiday: compassion, forgiveness, tolerance." Even with a ten year career, we see Perry continually finds himself regressing in the quality of his pictures to the point of critics mentioning his smile and bright teeth—something of a signature of past minstrel performers. In what other context of media or movie genre would a critic mention an actor's smile and that it "could be seen from space?" It is a description of not only the person, but their actions. If an actor allows themselves to be positioned in this manner, then a description such as this comes with the territory; we cannot expect someone to portray a certain image and not be classified as that very image by an onlooker who is also disappointed in the quality of the picture.

Films directed, produced, starring, and/or written by Tyler Perry

Rank	Title	Studio	Adjusted Gross	Release
1	Tyler Perry's Madea Goes to Jail	LGF	$105,256,900	2/20/09
2	Tyler Perry's Madea's Family Reunion	LGF	$80,641,800	2/24/06
3	Tyler Perry's Madea's Witness Protection	LGF	$67,512,900	6/29/12
4	Tyler Perry's Why Did I Get Married?	LGF	$66,999,700	10/12/07
5	Tyler Perry's Diary of a Mad Black Woman	Lions	$65,957,300	2/25/05
6	Tyler Perry's Why Did I Get Married Too?	LGF	$63,119,500	4/2/10
7	Tyler Perry's Madea's Big Happy Family	LGF	$55,271,600	4/22/11
8	Tyler Perry's Temptation: Confessions of a Marriage Counselor	LGF	$54,659,200	3/29/13
9	Tyler Perry's A Madea Christmas	LGF	$52,543,400	12/13/13
10	Tyler Perry's Meet the Browns	LGF	$48,815,400	3/21/08
11	Tyler Perry's The Family That Preys	LGF	$43,151,700	9/12/08
12	For Colored Girls	LGF	$39,628,000	11/5/10
13	Tyler Perry's Daddy's Little Girls	LGF	$38,068,900	2/14/07
14	Tyler Perry's Good Deeds	LGF	$36,904,200	02/24/12
15	Tyler Perry Presents Peeples	LGF	$9,650,900	05/10/13

This list illustrates the buying trends of the American audience towards Perry's works, as indicated, his top-grossing films feature Madea while roles such as *Alex Cross* ($25,888,412), *Tyler Perry Presents Peeples*, and *Tyler Perry's Family That Preys* are among those well below his average lifetime film earnings of $59,342,900.

Source: www.boxofficemojo.com, Acquired 2/18/2014

Perry's most popular and successfully marketed and profitable films to date have consisted of Madea themes, while many of his other films have paled in comparison in ticket sales and popularity, proving his core audience, and even those casual viewers, do not accept him stepping out of his gown and into more serious roles.

Because of Madea's popularity, it becomes obvious Perry has set a precedent and expectation for his fans, and when he deviates too far from that caricature, his bottom line reflects their displeasure. It is critical for Perry to change his themes because, not only has the Madea caricature been exhausted years ago, but also it clearly limits the effectiveness and reach he is able to have on a larger market. With the amount of influence and power Perry possesses, he is stifling his growth by committing himself to a caricature that audiences look to only for pure entertainment.

Conclusion

One of the glaring similarities I have found while doing research for this project is that most black directors have inserted their own personal experiences in their films. Such is the case with John Singleton's *Boyz N The Hood*, where he shot from South LA, a neighborhood he grew up near, comparable to Spike Lee's *Crooklyn*, which was loosely based upon his own life story. Their individual experiences shaped what they translated to the audience, and if not for that upbringing, we would not have the type of themes, quotes, and characters we now know. However, what made them great may have also contributed to what has stunted the growth and development of other directors.

As creative and demanding as Hollywood can be, it makes me contemplate whether directors have deliberately disregarded other genre-related projects such as Sci-Fi, mystery, action, etc. Sure there have been outliers and indie films which offer different perspectives and demonstrate creativity and ingenuity, however, the vast majority of major motion pictures from a black director are still influenced by Perry. It has been a successful run, but at what point does this act get old? If people are buying it, does that mean it is necessary? On a purely observational level, it appears as if black directors are not thinking abstractly enough to make a film such as *Avatar* (2009), *District 9* (2009), *Transformers* (2007), etc. I am not questioning their ability to think of and create blockbuster pictures but either they have become complacent with their talents or it is far more difficult than I have knowledge of for a black director to receive funding for a record-breaking motion picture in Hollywood. Regardless of the reason, there is a lapse in the amount of diversity in themes, and there is an insufferable amount of bland and predictable works that have lowered the bar for future black filmmakers.

In moving forward, we will continue to see blacks break down walls that were once reserved for whites only, as proof of the strides made in the last fifty years in politics, education, media, sports, and entertainment. Hopefully the structure of Hollywood is something that will also join the 21st century in producing works by blacks which express all different aspects of the human experience. Black filmmakers have been talented at their craft for nearly a century, and they are just now being recognized and supported for their endeavors. There is a battle in America between people who still hold onto the conservative beliefs of yesteryear and those who see our country for what it could be; this battle is far beyond politics and it surfaces itself in every facet of our culture.

Woody Allen and Martin Scorsese are both heralded as being great directors. Imagine if they were the only consistent directors of their time and only produced films about a particular subject or genre. No matter how great they are at filmmaking, it would eventually become stale and repetitive—that is the challenge of our contemporary black filmmakers. We are in a famine of talent from other filmmakers in the industry and because of Lee and Perry, it has resulted in a country of people who are satisfied with either education or entertainment and nothing in between. In the 80s and 90s, Lee pushed a black intellectual and socially conscious agenda; now we are seeing Perry use the bulk of his platform to continually promote slapstick entertainment, buffoonery, and lackluster comedies. According to ticket sales, neither are wrong. Publicity, along with exposure, is no fault of their own—but there is a clear gap in the amount of creativity and works blacks are producing in Hollywood. There are so many other categories of life black people can produce and create if given the chance, and it is a travesty to the American public we have been denied of such creativity and innovation. If we are not given the chance to produce more of our own works and continue to see a distorted view of ourselves, then we remain in this perpetual cycle in which outsiders believe a white woman who pretends to be black is actually "blacker" than someone she is pretending to be!

Hollywood is one of the slowest and conservative places in the country; contrary to popular belief, there is an image most actors, producers, and directors have to conform to in order to gain full support. After reading numerous books by black directors of the last fifty plus years, the story is common: they cannot get adequate funding to fully produce their films for the masses to view and support. Whether it is Keenen Ivory Wayans maxing out his credit cards to finance *Don't Be a Menace to South Central While Drinking Your Juice in the Hood*, Spike Lee having to plead with investors to get the money to finish *Malcom X* or *Fruitvale Station* needing additional funding to complete the film, it is no secret blacks have struggled to get anywhere in this country, even in mainstream society, but when one of us chooses to be as daring as a Hollywood director, resistance is to be expected. It is something I hope to see changed in the coming years as black people continue to move on to new ventures and successes.

I have a reserved optimism for the future, and I do believe it is possible for us to excel beyond prior expectations and open our own studios, like Lee and Perry have done. There is a new generation who understands how America works and is willing to work hard for what they want, and it is only a matter of time until we are able to make films that cover a wide range of topics and have the capacity to change the status quo.

Times have changed, Stepin Fetchit is no longer relevant amongst the common television viewer or movie-goer, but it seems Hollywood and American society, as a whole, have not matured to the point where they can accept a black figure without conforming to some former or outdated "coon" caricature.

There are no tap dancing Negro's on television today, Bill "Bojangles" Robinson is no longer dancing with Shirley Temple, and Paul Robeson would no longer have to hide the fact he was intellectual. While the landscape of American culture has become hyper-sensitive to anything remotely politically incorrect, the tone of African Americans in the arts is something which ebbs and flows almost at a laughable rate. On one hand, you can have political commentators such as David Freddoso who releases a book entitled *Gangster Government* (2011) with President Barack Obama on the cover. On the other hand, a print advertisement from Nivea featuring a clean shaven African American man holding a severed head of another black man with an Afro with the caption "Re-civilize yourself" is considered controversial and was protested and consequently taken down immediately. America has to choose which stereotypes we are willing to live with and which have no place in our democracy of free speech and "justice and liberty for all;" otherwise we will continue to see this inconsistent form of racial politics, which directly translates into the images we are presented on-screen.

That is the point of providing historical context and why it is necessary to mention the history of black films in America. At every point in history, the most popular films released, while largely fictional, were based upon what was occurring in the country. As we find ourselves now, the most popular and successful black director has found fame and fortune off of a cultural anachronism. It is remarkable to see the sharp decline and swift acceptability of our expectations of what passes as unofficially "black in America," and it only makes one wonder how much worse things will get before they get better. We, as a culture, have regressed to exactly what the NAACP stood up against in 1951, according to the protest featured earlier in the book, yet because Perry looks like us, there is no protest, no outcry, not even a peep. If we cannot look at ourselves objectively and see what we are being sold as opposed to who is selling it, we will continue to accept these forms of cultural degradation where we laugh at how we are portrayed, and everyone else will, too.

Stereotypical movies are not to blame for the disenfranchisement of blacks and neither are chauvinistic lyrics from rappers. We have, for many years, sought to point the finger at a single source as the answer to all of the tribulations and downfalls of African Americans. Social commentators have blamed rappers, buried the word "nigger," protested the release of movies which targeted blacks as secondary or inferior beings, made sagging jeans synonymous with juvenile delinquency, diagnosed black children with ADHD at a much higher rate than white counterparts, along with other generalized and knee-jerk reactions. While movies are an extension of reality, it is my belief all of these different things work together in the totality of what makes us the people we are. Mainstream America, and in some instances, blacks themselves, have made it all too easy to categorize and typecast themselves rather than accepting an individual with an independent thought process and true sense of self. Should black speakers assimilate the speech and rhetoric of MLK? Should female R&B artists mock the exact pitch and range of Whitney Houston? Should dancers have continued the exact moves of Fred Astaire or "Bojangles?" Should painters only look to Jean Michel Basquiat for influence? We cannot expect for a single source which defies expectations, to lead or be the standard for the rest of the population to assimilate the exact virtues of said individual. As great as Spike Lee is a director, would he have made *Higher Learning* (1997)? As talented as Tyler Perry has proved himself to be, could he have made *Soul Food* (1995)? Directors, just as any other industry in our country, have an obligation to their art. They produce works that challenge the very culture and psyche of their viewing public, and if everyone created *Do The Right Thing* movies or *Madea Goes to Jail* films, the industry would become diluted with an overabundance of thoughtless works not worth the film it is printed on.

The fact that there have been so many black directors who have created successful films is a testament to their resolve and creative genius. Statistically speaking, we are considered the minority in this country in nearly every category, except socially degenerative ones. When you consider the mounting expectations to produce something known to be untrue, as Keenen Ivory Wayans alluded to earlier, the allure of "selling out" becomes a very real temptation. Directors such as he should be saluted for their indelible influence on their audience and consequently the social consciousness of the world.

While Perry and Lee are the faces of black filmmaking, others have contributed to the culture through their own variations of creative projects which will eventually prove to be the standard for generations to come. When given the opportunity, we have seen the types of movies created by black filmmakers and the impact it has had on their community and our country. If filmmakers are denied the privilege of creating and publicizing their abilities and their craft, it not only destroys their will but it hinders the public's mental and social growth. Movies and television have been proven over time to influence our behaviors in real life and because of that powerful effect, it is that much more necessary for the public to be offered a variety of differing opinions, perspectives, value systems, and experiences. It is because of these things we must support the arts and aspiring creative minds who struggle to try to break through the glass ceiling of whatever industry they so choose. We, the people, are responsible for the messages presented, and if we value the culture, we have to be willing to stand behind it, even if it feels like we are standing alone.

Acknowledgements

F irstly, thanks to you for reading and allowing me to provide a different perspective of Tyler Perry's work thus far. If you enjoyed the read, please pass the word along to family and friends so we can broaden the discussion and bring more awareness to this issue. You could also leave reviews for the book as well, recommend your local bookstore have a book signing or carry this title. If you feel this subject is relevant and could be presented scholastically, recommend the title to a local university for course work or lecture series. While I spent over three years working on this project, it means nothing if the public is unaware of it and consciousness cannot spread; we must work together to spread the word one person at a time. Once again, thank you for your support and willingness to learn.

• Ezekiel J. •

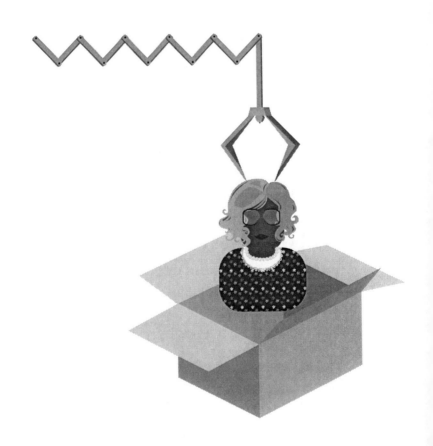

Bibliography

Chapter 1

1. Gregory, Dick. Lipsyte, Robert. Nigger: An Autobiography. Pocket Books, a division of Simon & Schuster, Inc. 1964. 204. Print.

2. Gregory, Dick. Lipsyte, Robert. Nigger: An Autobiography. Pocket Books, a division of Simon & Schuster, Inc. 1964. 155. Print.

3. Burke, Kerry, Mark Morales, Barbara Ross, and Ginger Otis. "Barneys Accused Teen of Using Fake Debit Card for $349 Belt Because He's a 'young Black American Male': Lawsuit." NY Daily News. N.p., 22 Oct. 2013. Web.

4. Lenin, D. Vladimir. Founder of the Russian Communist Party.

5. Alexander, George. Why We Make Movies: Black Filmmakers Talk About the Magic of Cinema. Harlem Moon Broadway, 2003. 40. Print.

6.   Alexander, George. Why We Make Movie: Black Filmmakers Talk About the Magic of Cinema. Harlem Moon Broadway. 2003. 511. Print.

7.   "Bank of America To Pay $335 Million Minority Loan Discrimination Settlement." *The Inquisitr News*. 22 Dec. 2011. Web.

8.   Pepitone, Julianne. "E-book Sales Top Paperbacks for First Time." *CNNMoney*. Cable News Network, 15 Apr. 2011. Web.

9.   Multiple authors. Stereotypes as Explanations: The Formation of Meaningful Beliefs about Social Groups. Cambridge University Press .2002. 2. Print.

10. Kaelber, Lutz. "North Carolina." *Eugenics in North Carolina*. University of Vermont, 21 Oct. 2012. Web.

11. Flood, Laura. "James Bond Switches to Heineken After $45M Deal." *Pastemagazine.com*. PasteMagazine, 21 Sept. 2012. Web.

12. Lee, Spike. Jones, Lisa. Uplift the Race: The Construction of School Daze. Fireside Books. 1988. 22. Print.

13. Wormser, Richard. "The Rise and Fall of Jim Crow." Woodrow Wilson. *PBS*. Web.

14. 66. Erik. "Product Placement in Pictures: Skyfall." *Brands And Films*. N.p., 4 Nov. 2012. Web.

15. Watkins, Mel. Stepin Fetchit: The Life and Times of Lincoln Perry. New York: Pantheon, 2005. 26. Print.

16. "Why The Amos 'n' Andy TV Show Should Be Taken Off The Air." NAACP Bulletin. 15 Aug. 1951. Web.

Bibliography

Chapter 2

1. Watts, Jill. Hattie McDaniel: Black Ambition, White Holly-wood. Quote by Clarence Muse entitled by "The Dilemma of the Negro Actor" Amistad Publishing. 2005. 76. Print.

2. Guerrero, Ed. Framing Blackness: The African American Image in Film. Temple University Press. 1993. 91. Print.

Chapter 3

1. Jay-Z. F.U.T.W. Magna Carta Holy Grail. Roc Nation.(2013)

2. DeMuth, Jerry. "Fannie Lou Hamer: Tired of Being Sick and Tired." *The Nation*. The Nation, 2 Apr. 2009. Web.

Chapter 4

1. Cole, J., and Young Jeezy. Kenny Lofton. 2013. MP3.

2. Alexander, George. Why We Make Movies: Black Filmmak-ers Talk About the Magic of Cinema. Harlem Moon Broad-way, 2003. 138. Print.

3. Nas. We're Not Alone. IDJ/Columbia Records. 2008. MP3.

4. Guerrero, Ed. Framing Blackness: The African American Image in Film. Temple University Press. 1993. 101. Print.

5. DuBois, W.E.B. The Souls of Black Folk. Dover Thrift Edi-tions 1903. 28. Print.

6. Guerrero, Ed. Framing Blackness: The African American Image in Film. Temple University Press. 1993. 75. Print.

7. Guerrero, Ed. Framing Blackness: The African American Image in Film. Temple University Press. 1993. 75. Print.

8. Guerrero, Ed. Framing Blackness: The African American Image in Film. Temple University Press. 1993. 74. Print.

9. Fox, Emily J. "Black Unemployment Rate Rises to 14.4% in June." *CNNMoney.* Cable News Network, 06 July 2012. Web.

Chapter 5

1. Boyz N The Hood. Doughboy.

2. Massood. Paula J. Black City Cinema: African American Urban Experiences in Film. Temple University Press. 2003. 147. Print.

3. Guerrero, Ed. Framing Blackness: The African American Image in Film. Temple University Press. 1993.

4. Guerrero, Ed. Framing Blackness: The African American Image in Film. Temple University Press. 1993. 30 Print.

5. Guerrero, Ed. Framing Blackness: The African American Image in Film. Temple University Press. 1993. 30 Print.

6. Alexander, George. Why We Make Movies: Black Filmmakers Talk About the Magic of Cinema. Harlem Moon Broadway, 2003. 151-152. Print.

7. Forbes. George Lucas. 14 Nov. 2014. Web.

8. "Films Such as 'Boyz' Presaged Rioting." *Baltimore Sun.* 08 May 1992. Web.

Bibliography

Chapter 6

1. West, Kanye. Clique. Island/Def-Jam. 2012.

2. Lee, Spike. That's my story and I'm Sticking to It. W.W. Norton & Company, Inc. pg. 2005. 38. Print.

3. Lee, Spike. That's my story and I'm Sticking to It. W.W. Norton & Company, Inc. pg. 2005. 144. Print.

4. Lee, Spike. Jones, Lisa. Uplift the Race: The Construction of School Daze. Fireside Books. 1988. 22. Print.

5. Lee, Spike. That's my story and I'm Sticking to It. W.W. Norton & Company, Inc. pg. 2005. 181. Print.

6. Lee, Spike. That's my story and I'm Sticking to It. W.W. Norton & Company, Inc. pg. 2005. 174. Print.

7. Lee, Spike. That's my story and I'm Sticking to It. W.W. Norton & Company, Inc. pg. 2005. 211. Print.

8. Fox, David J. "'Malcolm X': Excitement Is Building : Movies: Spike Lee's Film Opens Wednesday and a Lot Is Riding on How Broad Its Box-office Appeal Will Be." Los Angeles Times. 16 Nov. 1992. Web.

9. Cleaver, Eldridge. Soul on Ice. A Ramparts Book. 1970. 25-26. Print.

Chapter 7

1. Pimp C. Sippin On Some Sizzurp. Sony. 2005.

2. Harris-Perry. Melissa. Sister Citizen: Shame, Stereotypes, and Black Women in America. Yale University Press. 2011. 137-138. Print.

3. Harris-Perry. Melissa. Sister Citizen: Shame, Stereotypes, and Black Women in America. Yale University Press. 2011. 138-139. Print.

4. Bogle, Donald. Toms, Coons, Mulattoes, Mammies, and Bucks: An Interpretative History of Blacks in American Films. The Continuum International Publishing Group Inc. 2010. 67. Print.

5. Watkins, Mel. Stepin Fetchit: The Life and Times of Lincoln Perry. Books, New York: Pantheon, 2005. Print.

6. Gregory, Dick. Nigger: An Autobiography. Pocket Books, a division of Simon & Schuster, Inc. 1964. 26. Print.

7. Watkins, Mel. Stepin Fetchit: The Life and Times of Lincoln Perry. Books, New York: Pantheon, 2005. 13. Print.

8. Watkins, Mel. Stepin Fetchit: The Life and Times of Lincoln Perry. New York: Pantheon, 2005. 158. Print.

9. Watkins, Mel. Stepin Fetchit: The Life and Times of Lincoln Perry. New York: Pantheon, 2005. 56-57. Print.

10. Watkins, Mel. Stepin Fetchit: The Life and Times of Lincoln Perry. New York: Pantheon, 2005. 230. Print.

11. Bershad, Jon. Toure' Trashes Tyler Perry's Movies: "Cinematic Malt Liquor For The Masses." Mediaite.com. 20 Sep. 2011. Web.

12. Gane-McCalla, Casey. "Rev. Al Sharpton Calls Tyler Perry Critics "Proper Negroes"." News One RSS. N.p., 21 Oct. 2011. Web.

13. Watkins, Mel. Stepin Fetchit: The Life and Times of Lincoln Perry. New York: Pantheon, 2005. 204. Print.

Bibliography

14. Watkins, Mel. Stepin Fetchit: The Life and Times of Lincoln Perry. Books, New York: Pantheon, 2005. 5. Print.

15. Watkins, Mel. Stepin Fetchit: The Life and Times of Lincoln Perry. New York: Pantheon, 2005. 153. Print.

16. Watkins, Mel. Stepin Fetchit: The Life and Times of Lincoln Perry. New York: Pantheon, 2005. 148. Print.

17. Trotta, Daniel. "Zimmerman Case Was Not about Race, Juror Tells CNN." Reuters. 15 July 2013. Web.

18. "Spike Lee Talks About Tyler Perry's Filmmaking." Black Enterprise Entrepreneurs. YouTube. 29 Dec. 2009. Web.

19. "Tyler Perry: "Spike Lee can go straight to hell." *The Hollywood Reporter*. 19 April 2011. Web.

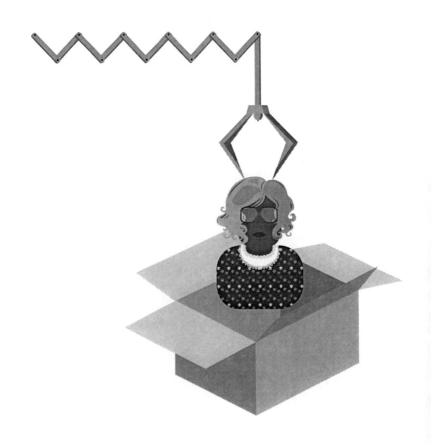

Biography

Ezekiel Walker

E zekiel is a writer in Durham, NC, who concentrates his efforts on non-fiction topics related to African American issues. He writes socially conscious works and is currently writing his third book. When he's not writing, he's rooting for the Los Angeles Lakers or watching a movie. His passion for watching films is evident in his latest book, *The Madea Factory*, in which he exhibits the knowledge he has gleaned from a lifetime of movie-going.

If a fellow writer asked me for advice, I would tell him to write what he wants and to never compromise his vision. This is a lesson I, myself, learned when soliciting traditional publishers for my second book *The Madea Factory*. I have been rejected numerous times. Each time it motivates me and confirms that not only is this book worthy of high consideration, but many persons are unaware of how to market a book with which they may not be comfortable. The issues presented in *The Madea Factory* may not be pleasant to talk about, but they are important. Working with Wisdom House Books has allowed me to stay true to my vision and to deliver this valuable and conscious work to a thoughtful and deserving audience.

In the spring of 2014, I self-published *The Madea Factory* alongside Wisdom House Books. I carried this book around in my head for three years, writing and rewriting often and informing my process by watching films from different periods in history, reading books on African American culture, and studying film genres and criticisms. The social concerns presented in this book stem from my passion for films, and the powerful effects a film can have on a person. I believe that directors have an unmatched power over mass audiences, and when that power is used to purport culturally questionable and inappropriate ideas, we as movie-goers must realize we have the power to control whether we support these obscene images.

The Madea Factory addresses many topics related to African

American stereotypes and images which are erroneously portrayed in the movie industry, largely by the most recognizable and profitable black filmmaker of all time, Tyler Perry. Perry's success comes at the huge expense of his own culture's progression and is reminiscent of the stereotypical and degrading characters that racist white directors once used to portray all black people. African Americans began performing and entertaining nationally over one hundred years ago, but now there is a division between the mainstream viewing public and the African American audience. This book provides clarity to why the gap continues to exist today and how it can best be overcome.

By noting legendary 20th century television and film personalities such as Stepin Fetchit, Paul Robeson, Hattie McDaniel and Lena Horne in order to comprehensively illustrate the persons who have paved the way for blacks in Hollywood today, I examine the ways in which Perry and his films actively undo their progress with every "Madea" movie ticket sold. Perry's presentations need to be acknowledged as the outdated and crass images they are. The African American demographic has worked for and deserves an image of ourselves that does not compromise our integrity, or the director's finances and relevance. My simple request is that Tyler Perry immediately cease directing, producing, and acting in films that derogatorily display blacks, and that audiences cease their support of these displays.

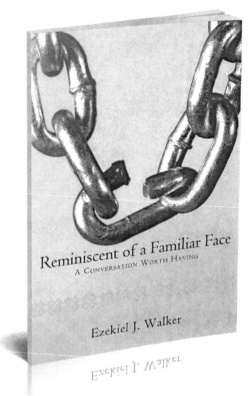

Discover another title by Ezekiel J. Walker
Reminiscent of a Familiar Face. (2010)

Connect with Me:
Find me at: www.themadeafactory.com
Friend me on Facebook: Ezekiel J. Walker
Find me on LinkedIn: Ezekiel J. Walker
Follow me on Twitter: @bookdontlie
Follow me on Instagram: @bookdontlie

CPSIA information can be obtained at www.ICGtesting.com
Printed in the USA
LVOW07s1659050315

429397LV00015B/131/P